Martial Rose Library
Tel: 01962 827306

D1494746

YVONNE GRACE

WRITING FOR TELEVISION:
SERIES, SERIALS AND SOAPS

creative ESSENTIALS

First published in 2014 by Kamera Books,
an imprint of Oldcastle Books,
PO Box 394, Harpenden, Herts, AL5 1XJ
www.kamerabooks.com

ISBN
978-1-84344-337-7 (print)
978-1-84344-338-4 (epub)
978-1-84344-339-1 (kindle)
978-1-84344-340-7 (pdf)

10
Typeset by Elsa Mathern in Franklin Gothic 9 pt
Printed and bound in Great Britain by 4edge Limited, Essex

To my dad. For all those Sunday dinner times; plates empty, we'd play 'Family Dictionary' – he'd get the book out – we'd all have to guess the word he was describing.

To my mum. For cooking all those Sunday dinners.

ACKNOWLEDGEMENTS

Thank you to the people who have influenced, helped, encouraged and inspired me along my career path:

Helen Greaves: for giving me my script editing break on *EastEnders*.
Hilary Salmon: for inspiring me, at the BBC, to work with writers.
Clive Brill: for allowing me creative reign as a development script editor at the BBC.
Tony Wood: for giving me my introduction to the Granada Television powerhouse.
Carolyn Reynolds: for teaching me how to be both creatively and commercially minded within ITV drama.
Russell T Davies: for teaching me how to construct, control and handle a storyline.
Kieran Roberts: for showing me how to be a good producer and believing in me.
Mal Young: for giving me responsibility, and then letting me lead, on the second series of *Holby City*.
Jonathan Powell: for showing me how to tackle the job of executive producer.

Here's to the writers that I have had the pleasure of working with and learning from: Tony McHale, Tony Jordan, Russell T Davies, Joe Turner, Sally Wainwright, Cath Hayes, Ashley Pharoah, Matthew Graham, Jeff Povey, Julie Rutterford, Jan McVerry, Jonathan Harvey.

And those that inspire and entertain me with their work: Lucy Gannon, Barbara Machin, Kay Mellor, Paul Abbott, Heidi Thomas, Ruth Jones, Chris Chibnall, Toby Whithouse, Bryan Elsley.

Thanks to William Gallagher for giving me the idea of writing a book about television writing in the first place, and then reading my early drafts.

And a special thanks to Jeff Povey, Debbie Moon, Glen Laker, Pete Lawson, Damon Rochefort, Lisa Holdsworth, Sally Abbott and Robert Goldsborough for their time and for sharing their television writing experiences with me.

CONTENTS

INTRODUCTION

So you are a writer. You love to tell stories and you have been scribing away for some time now and feel you are at the stage where you want to earn a living from your passion, the thing you like to do every day, because if you don't do it daily you are a nightmare to live with.

Television is an exciting, exacting, terrifying, funny, frantic, exposing and emboldening industry to work in. If you are lucky enough to land a regular writing position on a television drama, you will soon be enjoying good money and have the structure to your day you used to crave when you weren't a commissioned television writer. This structure will from now on be shaped by the rigours of the deadlines that will move into your house on the day of your first commission and take up residence in the dark space under your stairs. Deadlines are difficult house guests. They take over your space and hog the television – literally. So there are downsides.

Writing is a gruelling activity with the potential to batter you daily. It's a tough, scary thing to do, to begin crafting a narrative, creating characters and moving your plot line forward scene by scene through an hour of television. But you want to do this, you know it will be good for you; and, if you don't do it, you will regret it. Your headstone will read 'used to write, but life got in the way'. So do it you will. But working in such an exacting industry can and does make you feel really rubbish about yourself and your writing ability. You need a thick(ish) skin, the resilience of a plastic stacking chair and a self-belief as flexible and strong as a bungee to really be happy working in television.

You may hope to work on an already established series or serial, or join the stable of writers on a soap, or you may be holding out for the elusive joy of writing your own single, or serial, for television and no doubt have already cast this and sourced where the wrap party will be. We've all done it. I still do. Whichever case scenario fits you, be certain that with this holy grail comes a lot of fuss, bother and what my nanna used to call histrionics.

In this book I am going to show you how to avoid too many histrionics, and to point out the skills necessary to get on in television as a writer, the pitfalls to avoid and the attitudes and mindset to adopt in order not only to succeed in getting through the television door but also to make sure it doesn't whack you in the bum on the way out.

HOW IT ALL STARTED

Wendy Richard is staring at me. She has her hand on her hip and she is pulling the sort of face my Uncle George would say was like 'a bulldog chewing a wasp'. I am in trouble and I know it and she knows it. There are three other script editors in the office, Barbara, Colin and Hattie, and they are staring at me too – all of them without exception thinking 'thank God it's not me'. I stare back at Wendy. Hard. I swear I can hear Hattie snort a nervous laugh back up her nose whilst Colin tries to do a very good impression of a radiator.

'Well?' Wendy's gimlet stare takes no prisoners. 'Yes?' I answer querulously. 'Where the fuck is my script?' repeats Wendy, her expression now synonymous with the one Pauline Fowler gave her tumble dryer when it broke down: irritation, frustration and a huge dollop of pure anger.

Another seemingly endless pause during which, out of the heat of mental and physical paralysis that has overcome me since Wendy invaded my private space, an idea begins to form of what I could say to alleviate this situation –

'Go away.'

Yes. I said that. I had other, more complex thoughts, like a pretty detailed explanation of why her script was late finding its way to her pigeon hole in the green room (I couldn't sign off on the rehearsal script until my producer had okayed the last changes, and she couldn't do that until she had read and done the same on the episode before mine, which she couldn't do until the rewrites for the previous ep had come in, and they were due that morning, but we had just heard that the writer had had to go to a funeral, so we were actually about to have a meeting to finish the scene after the second ad break so we could push the whole thing forward), but I didn't say any of that because I told Wendy Richard – matriarch of the most successful soap on telly – to go away.

It was like farting before the Queen. You just didn't do it.

A BEGINNING – THE DEPTFORD WIVES

How I got to be in that place, standing on that hideous carpet, breathing the rarefied air of an outraged actress, is a rather circuitous story.

I started out, with a degree in theatre design under my belt, by totally avoiding the rigours of designing exciting sets for the stage. Instead I acted on them, for five years, until I realised it wasn't speaking the story that interested me; it was creating stories and working with those who wrote them.

The written word has always held a fascination and the whole business of storytelling – why writers write like they do, what makes a good script great and how you change a mediocre drama into a fabulous one – are the questions I have pretty much busied myself with ever since.

I ran a script development company back in the early nineties in Deptford, South London. We were called the Deptford Wives. And the script-in-hand readings we did on the dusty old stage in the back room at the Birds Nest pub were always really lively, funny affairs and lots of people came (even from north of the river) to see what we were doing.

A mixed bag of humanity used to pack out the theatre. Some were actors or writers, others were agents, and there were a few radio producers, television producers and script editors. The bar during the interval was populated by professionals and non-professionals in and on the fringes of the storytelling industry. Rubbing shoulders with the great and the good of television, radio and theatre were Deptford's finest: Charlie the drunk (who thought he was Rudolph Valentino),

Martin the landlord's mother (who was terrifying and wore lilac-tinted specs with lenses the size of tupperware lids), Blonde Gloria (the door girl) who wore cowboy boots and oversized man sweaters, and my friend Vania and I, trying to act professional and sometimes pulling it off.

It was a crush but a productive one on every level. The professional types were there to look out for fresh talent and champion the new voices of the time. The non-professionals were picking up tips and making connections, and the drunks and locals were enjoying the camaraderie and getting drunk. Which we all were to a greater or lesser extent.

Back in 1990, networking was reserved for high-flying CEOs and people who knew their way around a spreadsheet. But standing on the sticky carpet, inhaling the fug of a busy, jolly pub in full swing, chatting and laughing and generally having fun, I was doing just that, and with people whom I would ultimately need to give me a leg up into an area I knew little about but wanted to be part of. It was working. It just didn't feel like it. That's what networking should feel like for you, too.

KNOCKING ON DOORS

When I was knocking on doors, it seemed the BBC was staffed by Oxbridge graduates; coming from a polytechnic and having a strong northern accent rather pushed my ginger noggin over the parapet. However, I was tenacious, confident and kept firing off letters with my CV attached (and following this up with phone calls) to drama producers in the serial department like Phillippa Giles and in drama series like Helen Greaves, Jane Harrison, Leonard Lewis, Mervyn Watson and Clive Brill.

These names have either completed world domination now or gone off to do different things, but then, back in the late 1980s, I needed these people to be accessible and open and to at least see me. So I could impress them. With my amazing knowledge of what was great on television and what dramas did not work. I had tons of opinions. Tons of passion and drive. I could talk your leg off about why *Oranges Are Not the Only Fruit* was the best thing on telly and how I could show the BBC how to fix *Eldorado*.

Fortunately, the likes of Phillippa Giles listened to me. And she had a friend working on *EastEnders* who needed a seriously strong script team behind her. Her friend was Helen Greaves and I became one of the seriously strong script team.

We all need a champion, someone who doesn't mind sharing their experience and expertise with you – this is a vital relationship to nurture if you are to make it in television. We don't all have a hugely successful person in whose slipstream we can sail through the doors of the big indies or the BBC, but we do, all of us, have at our disposal our talent, our personality, our personal opinions and our networking opportunities.

KEY PEOPLE USEFUL TO KNOW IN TELEVISION – AND WHO YOU WANT TO KNOW ABOUT YOU

Television, unlike the world of film, is a producer-led genre (which isn't, of course, to ignore the commissioners, the creative directors, the controllers of channel. No, I do not intend to offend). However, after what seems (to me) like rather futile analysis, I have decided not to include specific names and titles. This is because television, like a lot of high-octane creative and commercial businesses, moves at a fast pace and I do not want to do the unthinkable and date this book (I would hate to be 'last season'). So I will keep this section general and give you instead a general lowdown on the responsibilities of executive producers, producers, and development producers/script editors.

EXECUTIVE PRODUCER

To make your life more complicated than it no doubt already is (trying as you are to scale the slippery shingle of television drama production), the people with whom you will want to make contact do not, unfortunately, all share the same (or even in some cases remotely similar) job title. What moniker they adopt depends on the company or channel they work for.

A rule of thumb, however, is that if a producer has 'executive' before their name they are likely to be directly responsible for the look, content, tone and cost of the dramatic output of the show in question.

A good executive is both a diplomat and a creative. They are politically savvy, by which I don't mean that they could win a debate in the House of Commons, but rather that they are political on a personal management level, with a very strong creative and editorial track record.

Executives have to detect, deal with and solve all manner of problems arising during not only the day-to-day, but also, if their drama is a series or serial, the year-on-year running of their drama.

When addressing the issue of writers on their show, the executive producer will not only want to use the best names available, but also add to their stable. This is because executive producers know (especially on established long runners like *Casualty* or *Holby City*) how fast their writer turnaround can be. It's a television truism that, no matter how keen, or experienced, or just downright hard working they are, writers do get burnt out if they are overcommissioned and over-relied upon to deliver. A good executive, then, will want to be made aware of new writers and to get a handle on new work.

Not all execs are the same and not all work within a system that allows this, but I was lucky, and in my own experience as an executive producer I had access to, and actively encouraged, new writers and new ideas. I had a development team under me at Carlton Television and it was to these development script editors that writers and their agents would come. A development script editor's main job is to bring new talent into the department/company and they may even be working on specific initiatives set up by the channel or company.

Most executive producers would pass you on to their producer should you contact them directly. However, it is the executive producer who will ultimately have the last say on whether your scripts fit the bill or not. And it is this signature you most want to secure on your writing contract. So find out who this person is and then focus your efforts on those who work for them.

PRODUCER

And so we come to the producer. It's a great role. It's a hard role. I have happily enjoyed my years as a television producer (my liver didn't so much), and I can honestly say that my enjoyment has been largely due to the casts, crews, writers and script teams I have had the fortune either to find or to aquire. Without the commitment and talent of these amazing people, a producer has a hard, and perhaps even impossible, task ahead of them. It is true to say that you are only as good as the people you surround yourself with, and in television this is truer than ever.

A producer's responsibility is directly to the programme, or block of episodes to which they are assigned. They must construct and deliver an entertaining, engaging, audience-savvy, quality dramatic product under usually impossible deadlines, restricted budgets and exacting requirements from their channel, company or department executives.

Not all producers are the same (why would they be?) but most, in my experience, range from being slightly interested in to massively obsessed with storylines, story creation, writers, writing and scripts in general.

A producer worth their salt will want to be aware of any new talent and will positively encourage their script teams to find this new blood. Addressing your opening gambit to the producer of a drama you admire will not offend, but you will usually find that your details have been passed on to a script editor. This is no bad thing. A long-running programme like *Holby City*, *Casualty*, *Doctors* or one of the soaps needs imagination, talent and creativity to keep it fresh and relevant to the huge audiences that keep tuning in, and one of the jobs a script editor does is help find that talent for the greater good of their show and the department they work in.

And I don't just want to mention soaps or series here; the quality of the serials and shorter-run formats coming out of both the BBC and ITV is exceptional at the moment. Producers are largely responsible for the quality of the scripted drama they control and a writer-savvy, story-led producer is, in my view, the very best sort of creative working in a management role.

So familiarise yourself with who these people are and watch the shows they make with a critical eye of appraisal. If you contact a producer directly and actually begin a dialogue, rather than being passed on to someone else, you must show you have your own opinions and an ability to back them up.

Television loves an opinion well presented. A large part of the 20 years I have been involved in drama production for television has been spent forming, holding and voicing my opinions on what is made, what should be made and how it should be made.

When you come into contact with people who can make your writing life in television not only happen in the first place, but also (happily) continue, make sure you have some solid opinions, not just about your own work, but on past and current television drama output.

DEVELOPMENT PRODUCER/DEVELOPMENT SCRIPT EDITOR

Again, depending on whom a particular development person works for, the titles may differ. However, the jobs have an overall similarity. I was a development script editor at the BBC when *Eldorado* was their 'Marmite' series (you either loved it or hated it) and my job was specifically to find and develop good, commercial, entertaining, high-quality, dramatic series treatments for BBC1, which I would ultimately pitch at the department's regular development meetings. Times change and so do corporations and the way they work internally. Nevertheless, there are still initiatives within the BBC for new writers, and more about that later.

Development script editors have overall responsibility for bringing new writers into the department/company and presenting their work to their producers and exec producers. They are keen to champion writers and their ideas at development meetings and it is in the development script editor's interest not only to actively encourage the introduction of new writers and new voices to their department but also to nurture their writer's progress.

A good development script editor will use social networking sites, go to the theatre, listen to radio and watch a lot of television. They are looking for the next new voice and for a particular spark of talent and originality. If your genre is not television and you come to their attention via another media, they will want to believe that you can make the crossover. A good development person has insight, initiative and a strong creative sense of not only what makes a great script, but also which writers would suit their programme or fit their department's requirements.

Do your research. Find out who the development script editors are and contact them. You have scripts you have written, you believe in yourself as a writer, and in your voice, you believe you have something to say – make sure the development script editor hears you. Be tenacious. Be polite.

CONTACTING PEOPLE YOU WANT TO HELP YOU

Contacting people you want to help you in your writing career is a vital part of promoting yourself and your talent. You must, however, do this in a consistently polite, friendly, open way and avoid at all times being overly familiar, intense, flippant or just generally annoying.

You can send a direct message to those who are following you on Twitter, but unless you are lucky enough to have a key drama person following you I recommend you email them. Twitter is a tricky place to do first contacts; it tends to be a more chatty, convivial place whereas the most effective meet-and-greet messages are more measured, not restricted to 140 characters and a little more formal in tone.

THINGS TO GET RIGHT ALL THE TIME IN EMAILS

- Get the name, the spelling of the name and the position the recipient holds in the company correct.

- Keep the email short, sweet and succinct.

- Ask if they would like to read your script (and give them your pithy, powerful, engaging logline), say you have the treatment ready to read – or, indeed, the full script if they would like that instead.

- Having offered the goods, it may sound obvious, but ensure you have actually completed both the treatment and the script to the highest standard. No point in crashing something out in haste if your work is requested and you have to deliver.

- If your work is requested, respond professionally and do not go over the top in your eagerness to please. And give them only what they ask for. A treatment, an outline, or the script itself. Never send more than one piece of work. Unless asked for it.

- Leave it a couple of weeks minimum. Then chase up, but always in a friendly, open, easy manner.

AGENTS: WHERE TO FIND THEM AND WHAT THEY SHOULD DO FOR YOU

It is a prickly truth that, if you do not have an agent but want to be taken seriously as a writer, and are keen to work within the media industry doing just that, you are in a catch-22 situation.

When I was starting out in the television industry, it was still possible to encourage new writers, literally fresh out of the theatre or having just written a radio play, into the world of television writing. These writers did not, in the main, have agents as they were very new to the writing world, and it was the support of script editors like myself, going to the theatre, listening to radio drama and taking note of writers whose work we liked, that often resulted in very inexperienced writers being thrown in at the deep end of, for example, *EastEnders*. This may or may not have been a good thing; there were quite a few writers who crashed and burned via this high-octane introduction to television drama writing. But, for a healthy number of writers, this opportunity was all the leg-up they needed to get started, get confident and get commissioned.

And, even before I started in television drama as a script editor, I had the enviable job of being a sort-of writer talent scout for Channel Four, which involved going to lots of fringe theatre plays all over London, and listening to the radio, and generally getting acquainted with who was writing what and then telling Allon Reich about them. (This was all before he started producing and exec producing a clutch of some of the best British films of the last ten years.) But the fact that there was such an opportunity for me, and for writers in general, to do this sort of thing proves just how different the landscape looks now.

WEIGHING UP THE AGENT ISSUE

Most production companies, including ITV and the BBC, do not accept unsolicited scripts. The BBC Writersroom accepts work from non-represented writers (more about them a little later) but there is no equivalent within ITV production. So it is important to get an agent as this makes it much easier to get through doors in the first place. Right? Well, yes. To a point.

I want to add a note of caution. Do not rush too quickly into the process of acquiring an agent. You need to be ready yourself. In terms of your outlook, your career path, your own confidence as a writer, and in the work you are producing.

There is a lot of discussion about agents on the Internet. Writers blog about them, their merits are discussed in forums, and writers celebrate online when they've found one to represent them. However, there is also a strong school of thought that supports the viewpoint that an agent is not the solution to all writer problems. To an extent, this is true.

Unlike the Fairy Godmother in *Cinderella*, an agent isn't someone who will appear when you are feeling down and make it all right by waving a magic wand. I would like that to be the case, especially if she or he were to sing 'Bibbity Bobbity Boo' whilst doing so, but, of course, that would be inappropriate.

An agent will help you get work by representing your talent where you cannot, but you must also do the legwork and make contacts yourself.

Production companies, commissioners, script editors, directors and producers expect the writers whose work they make/commission/work on to have an agent. If you do not have one, then the chances are that these key people, essential to your advancement in the world of drama on the small screen, will not be familiar with your work. That is why contacting the development people, the script editors and those whose job it is to be aware of your talent and your existence is vital.

Be proactive. Writing, in the main, is a solo activity. Being successful as a writer takes an inclusive, collaborative approach from you.

All is not lost if you do not have an agent when you are starting out. There are things you can do yourself. Get busy online. Go to script festivals and participate in screenwriting forums. Promoting yourself and your work is no longer considered 'bad form'. Use the social media at your disposal to your own advantage. In this way, you open up your options and chances of gaining writing work via connections with organisations or individuals that you have made online, or in a gathering of like-minded people.

This may or may not be paid and, if the latter, it is up to you whether you choose to do it; but, either way, having done the work you can now say you are a writer – a working writer. This elevates you from the position of being someone who writes but, as yet, does it for themselves.

Baby steps. Nurture your ability and don't throw your talent out there for just anyone to grab hold of. Your creative ability is precious and you need to grow, not only in skill, but also in confidence, in order to do yourself and your writing justice when you do gain writing work.

If, however, you are starting out and do have an agent, having only written a couple of scripts, then you are either very lucky, or with the wrong agent. I say this because acquiring an agent is a two-way process. You need the professional clout they can give you, but remember that they also need your talent and will take a cut of anything you earn. The relationship therefore has to be symbiotic, not parasitic. The respect must be mutual and those on both sides of this delicately balanced coin must be happy.

If an agent has taken you on in a wink having read a script and said they liked it, they may (I hedge my bets here) just be after a quick buck. And, if they don't get it from you, they're going to leave you pretty much languishing in the lower drawer of their client cabinet whilst they focus their attention on the bigger cash earners elsewhere.

So do your research on the agents that you meet and have meetings with. Like most things in life, it is better to be informed than ignorant.

GETTING PROFESSIONAL HELP

Be sure you have made your work as good as it can be. It involves a financial outlay, but I would recommend you invest in getting good, professional editorial help with your drafts as you write them. There are plenty of good mentors/script editors out there with their own websites; some are more expensive than others and offer slightly different services but, in my view, you get what you pay for. Look at the experience the script editor outlines on their website and read recommendations if they are available and get second opinions if you can.

Here is the address that will take you straight to the services page of my website: *http://scriptadvice.co.uk/scriptadvice_services.html*

Having said that most companies do not accept unsolicited scripts, Hayley McKenzie, script editor and head girl at Script Angel, a very good mentoring website for writers, has a list of those that do: *http://scriptangel.wordpress.com/2013/01/17/production-companies-uk-accepting-unsolicited-scripts/*

Bear in mind that this is a link to Hayley's blog, and that neither she nor I can personally recommend these production companies. If you decide to contact them, do your research. Make sure your script matches the genre they are keen on developing (some have restrictive areas of development) and follow their submission rules carefully.

One way of getting feedback that you don't have to pay for is to approach the BBC Writersroom (*http://www.bbc.co.uk/writersroom/*). You don't need an agent to have your script read by this department. There's a waiting list (obviously), but here's Paul Ashton, latterly of the Writersroom, now at Creative England, telling me what will make a script stand out:

> We are looking for a spark of talent, it might be raw and it need not be polished, but they must be doing something in the work that engages us. We are looking for strength of voice, individuality of voice, strength of perspective/POV, a real imperative to tell stories for an audience, an ambition in what they do. We're not looking for more of the same – we look for what's different, surprising, unusual, innovative, irrepressible.

Taken from the BBC Writersroom website, here is some information on the Shadow Schemes, their initiative for writers keen to work on the bigger, long-running shows (*Casualty*, *Holby City*, *Doctors* and *EastEnders*). You do need to be represented to be eligible.

Shadow Schemes

The Shadow Schemes are a way to mirror the show's writing process by producing an episode from which the writer will be assessed for a commission. We'd like writers to learn the necessary skills on how to write for the shows, as we've discovered from the success of the Writers Academy that fewer writers failed on their first commission because of the training they received. So there will be a little training to include writers' workshops, lectures and exercises on storytelling and the show format. The writers will have a formal induction on the show, including a set tour, and then they'll be taken through the script development process. On each show the trial process will vary. We are aiming to run one Shadow Scheme for each show over the course of the year but there may be opportunity to run more.

Writer Recruitment

Participation on one of the Shadow Schemes is by selection. We have an established central database for writer recruitment across all four shows and we only accept scripts submitted via agents. We read and consider scripts for the shows, and recommend accordingly. When submitting, agents should send one original piece that best illustrates their client's ability to write for our shows and tell us which series the writer is most keen to work on.

It is also a good idea to buy the current *Writers' and Artists' Yearbook*, and their website is a useful source of information and help: *http://www.writersandartists.co.uk/*

Amongst the many literary agencies promoting the work of writers in all genres I would start with a small list of some of the best, with which you may want to get acquainted:

Curtis Brown: *http://www.curtisbrown.co.uk*
MBA: *http://www.mbalit.co.uk/*
David Higham: *http://www.davidhigham.co.uk/*
Blake Friedmann: *http://www.blakefriedmann.co.uk/*
Dench Arnold: *http://www.dencharnold.com/contact.asp*

Remember: do not rush in too quickly or too soon to get an agent. Hone your authorial voice and get to know yourself and the work you're writing, or want to write, before you start promoting yourself as someone who needs representation.

And, when you feel you *are* ready, remember that an agent should:

• Make you feel good about your work and confident in your talent

• Be good at networking and actually do a fair amount of it

• Get you contacts you could not get yourself in the industry, with script editors, producers and production companies

• Spread your name around at networking occasions and generally within the industry as someone with talent who is not only available for work but also pursuing their own projects

• Represent you and your talent in a professional, approachable and enthusiastic manner

Your agent can also help in an editorial fashion, highlighting the strengths of your work and pointing out where they feel you may need development. This should be done constructively.

The agent that doesn't actively do the above isn't worth the cut you negotiated. Be fair but tough and, if it's not working out, say your farewells and move on.

Good luck with your search and, above all, remember that talent and self-belief are a powerful combination – and that you will need both to get into, and get on in, the television writing industry.

THE DNA OF A TELEVISION WRITER

Nothing worth doing is easy in my view, and working as a television writer takes a certain type of person and certain type of writer.

The route in will not, in all likelihood, be straightforward, and at some stage you are going to need a champion. So you need to nurture that potential champion amongst the people you meet and in the connections you make.

You need to network. Embrace Twitter and Facebook. I was a latecomer to the whole social network thing – but, now that I'm cosily settled there, I rather like it and can see just how much easier it is for writers to make good connections and develop good relationships via their tweets and posts and via the groups they choose to join. Join writing forums and LinkedIn – spread your net wide and utilise anyone and everyone you meet on these networks to connect with like-minded folks and those actually working in television.

Making fortuitous connections on the Internet is a bit like dating (without the snogging). As with dating, you should be cautious but confident – find out about the person you are connecting with and do not rush in with 'Can you read my script for me?' You wouldn't beg your date to marry you first time around, would you? *Would you?* Do not rush the person you want to help you. Take your time and be honest and open about what you want to achieve. People will respect you for it and, in my experience, those who genuinely love their jobs are never reticent about talking about it to someone who is interested.

Connecting is a personal and a political thing to do. Do it with focus and humanity and you won't go far wrong.

RESPECT THE INPUT OF OTHER PROFESSIONALS

Once through the door of the production office on your television drama of choice (or that of someone else's choice), put your ego away and get ready to learn stuff. Writing drama for television is a team effort and being good at it, and happy whilst doing it, all depends on how easy you are to work with and how ready you are to write like the wind and write well whilst doing so. The script editors, storyliners (if the show has them), story editor (most returnable series have these), production assistants, producer and director are there to help you get the best out of yourself and your script. It is not in their interest to upset you, confuse you or disrespect your input, and it is not in your interest to be difficult at any stage of the writing and re-writing process – mutual respect at all times.

COLLABORATE

Very important. Be someone who can collaborate with the various people you will meet along the way as you write your first, second, third and (rarely) fourth draft. Be ready to make changes at the last minute and do not hold on to your baby. Once you have delivered to deadline, it is not yours, it belongs to the show, and now you have made it perfect as only you can you must let it go. The show will love you and you will get to write more.

BE COMMERCIALLY AWARE

Storytelling is at the root of everything we do. But, in television, so is commercialism. I like the marriage between these two – but if you are the sort of writer who believes in the rarity and preciousness of their storytelling skill, then I would say telly is not for you. Dramatic writing for the television can be compared, quite healthily in my view, to making a product – making stuff – within an industrial setting. Writing on a show like *EastEnders* or *Holby City* (though both shows have different format lengths and differing budgets) is like working at the epicentre of a huge story factory. Your input as a writer is essential and required regularly, and the producers will demand that you are consistently creative and inventive with both your storyline pitches and character ideas, armed with which they will expect you to come, bristling, to the Story Conference table, on average once every three months.

As a writer on a long-running show, you will have to get used to coming up not only with story ideas that are dismissed at first outing, but also those that are jumped on with vigour and then discussed, re-shaped and packaged up in a story document that you might not even recognise when it pings into your inbox on that happy day when you are commissioned to write an episode featuring the very storyline you came up with in embryo on the day of the Story Conference.

Get used to thinking of your audience and their reaction to and engagement with your stories. Although some series are issue-based, the majority of returnable series depend on the depth and quality of the characters and the amount of emotion you can find within a storyline.

BE INCLUSIVE WITH YOUR IDEAS AND YOUR PROCESS

I believe the best television writers are fantastically flawed people – those that can draw on the oodles of mistakes, public humiliations, downright bad behaviours, tacky decisions, and pure and simple dumb things they have done to make their storylines ring true, their characterisation credible and their audience ultimately engage with their creations.

Be ready to share your experiences and do not shy away from allowing others their input into your story ideas. Russell T Davies created *Revelations*, a 26-part x 25 minute soap (or series) for the ITV network, and, as the script editor at Granada, which was making the show (on a laughably small budget), I was expected to come up with enough story material to fill those episodes and do it in record time – thus ensuring the production could begin shooting in order to hit the alarmingly tight transmission deadline. All of it fast, all of it frantic, and all of it very, very funny. After Russell, Paul Marquess and

I emerged from our stuffy story office at the end of the storylining day, there wasn't a secret left between us or an idea left on the table. You wash your dirty laundry in public when you're strapped for time and storyline, and long-running shows gobble up time and story. Be inclusive, be open, be accessible.

BE RELIABLE

By this I don't mean stand your round in the bar after a day's filming, or after a gruelling edit session – although this is, by the way, a good idea. I mean be the sort of writer that the script team and the producer know always delivers.

An average returning series can have anything from 10 to 20 writers on its books; and, of these writers, a select group of between 5 and 10 (if the producer is lucky) are the ones the script team consistently go to for a solid, trouble-free commission. Reliability doesn't mean being a predictable writer, but it does mean being the sort who embraces the rigours of that particular show, not only writing a fresh episode every time, but delivering it on time.

BE GOOD AT MEETING DEADLINES

Some writers don't react well to deadlines.

A writer I once had the misfortune of using on *Holby City* consistently refused to say when his draft would land on the metaphorical script mat. With the whistle blowing loudly in all our ears and the wire practically cutting our throats, he always did manage to deliver a great episode eventually. However, the pain of the wait and the stress this put the team under meant that it was only just worth it. I spoke to his wife once, who clearly hadn't been briefed as to a plausible story to roll out should the production office call and blithely responded to my queries with 'X is walking the dog. Who shall I say called?' 'The producer of *Holby City*,' I replied. I don't think she breathed much during the next exchange. I said that his episode was due today and that I was paying a director to play golf as he didn't have a script to prepare for shooting. There was an infinitesimal pause and then she said, 'But he's back now and just shut the study door.' I had no reason to doubt her.

But, if you are the sort of writer who wants to stay in telly, it's all so much easier if you can continue grasping the nettle that got you there in the first place – and this means being able to deliver on deadline. Leave the dog walking to your wife/partner; or, when the commission at last arrives, get rid of the dog?

Mal Young (my executive producer on *Holby City*) once snorted with derision when I said that, although I was currently single, I was hopeful of climbing off the shelf soon. I do not quote him directly, but he said something like, 'Producers don't have time for a shag, let alone a relationship.' He was, by the way, in the main, right. So take your life, put it on hold and deliver your script to deadline – it's the least you can do, because your producer is gagging for a social life and won't be able to so much as slap on a bit of lippy unless you deliver your promised draft. Think of it, as the date draws nearer and you are still struggling with the pesky storyline, as an act of charity.

TAKE NOTES WELL

His name shall remain a smudged secret here – he has some influential friends and I don't want any unpleasantness – but do not, under any circumstances, do as a writer I was once script editing did: turn up without his own copy of the script and just a pencil tucked behind his ear.

His eyes were rolling in his head from, I guessed, last night's excesses and, when they stopped rolling, I saw they were also bloodshot. I was green and inexperienced; he knew it and I knew it, but I held my ground. We went through the script line by painful line – mainly because I, in my nervousness, had started talking slooowly, as if I was addressing a stroke victim. He became more defensive as the session progressed and eventually, when I think neither of us could have stood another tense minute, snapped his pencil in half with the effort of trying to write legibly. He stared at me – eyes like pebbles at the bottom of a fish tank – and said, 'C***.'

Needless to say, I ended the session pretty swiftly, reported him to my producer and he didn't come back to the show.

So do, by all means, celebrate your commission and raise a glass or two, but do it well before you have an edit session and always come prepared; not just with script and writing utensil, but with the mental attitude that your script won't be right at first or second draft, but that, maybe by the third, you'll be on the home stretch.

In television – especially on series and serial television – it will seem that everyone, even the woman who comes round with the tea trolley, will have not only an opinion on, but also some input into, your script. Well, woman with the tea trolley aside, this is actually true. Depending on the show you are writing, you may have to go through the notes and opinions of:

- the executive producer
- the producer
- the series script editor
- the story producer
- the script editor

And, in some cases, these scripty types can look very young – which is because they are occasionally grabbed wet from university to do the job. Taking notes from someone young enough to be your son or daughter can be arduous but necessary; just remember that the recent embryo with the serious expression and highlighter pen hovering over your precious cliffhanger can make your passage tricky or easy – it's up to you.

Taking notes is hard, though. No doubt about it. Especially when you have comments like 'This is funny, but can you make it funnier?' ringing in your ears. And I for one, speaking as a seasoned script editor myself, do not enjoy the oft-repeated note, 'The dialogue is too on the nose.'

But I can say that, for most of the time, and for most of your career as a writer in telly, you will be blessed with script editors who know their stuff and can convey their opinions to you without making you wince.

DO NOT BEAR GRUDGES AND
DO NOT TAKE REJECTION PERSONALLY

This is another toughie. On a series or serial, where you are required to write an episode that relates in some way to the episode before and the one that will follow, you may find that, although you think your script is perfect, the production may see it another way. Take a deep breath – carry on writing and the next one will probably be held up as a fine example of how the show should be written. The odds are that you and the people paying you will often have differing opinions – but, hey, telly is subjective and we all need to keep our feet on the ground.

Accolades are great, but rejection may be around the corner – treat them both the same and carry on being a great telly writer.

THE SKILLS YOU NEED
TO BE A TELEVISION WRITER

Firstly, a couple of definitions:

Series: A drama that is open ended. A core cast of returning characters. The backdrop remains the same and is returned to each week. This is also called the 'precinct'. There may be several stories per episode which are resolved, but the series storyline, that which is carried by the core returning cast, remains open. For example: *Waking the Dead*. *Coronation Street*. *Downton Abbey*. *Scott and Bailey*. *Skins*.

Serial: A drama of more than one or two parts with a strong serial element. A core cast of returning characters and an over-arching storyline, but in this case the storyline is ultimately resolved. For example: *The Wrong Mans*. *Being Human*. *My Big Fat Teenage Diary*. *Peaky Blinders*.

WATCH A LOT OF TELEVISION

Work out what it is you like about a particular programme and why. If you like the soaps, ask yourself which is your favourite and why this is so. The answer you give will be the immediate, knee-jerk reason. This will be the strongest aspect of the show that is speaking to you.

This impact is important to register as a 'punter' because, as a professional television writer, you will need to recognise, understand and recreate that impact on your audience, via your writing.

STUDY THE DIALOGUE AND CHARACTERISATION ON SCREEN

Television is a visual medium and the narratives are carried, in the main, by dialogue and characterisation. Practise your skills in both – you will need to be really good at these tricky areas of storytelling for the screen if you are, firstly, to be noticed and, secondly, commissioned.

PRACTISE STORYLINING

To make it an easier ride for yourself writing for series and serials, you will need to get good at thinking of stories not just in terms of three main drama beats, or acts, as is traditionally the case, but in terms of multiple layers and many beats. A simple character arc, or long view, from A to Z, is essential: mark this out and know it well. However, the points between A and Z will be many and varied and depend on the relationships contained within this arc, as well as those of the other core characters in your story.

PLAY WITH STRUCTURE

Get really good at setting your storylines into a solid, workable framework. Structure is everything in television scripts. Some writers I have worked with on shows like *EastEnders* and *Holby City* have found the strict rigours of the script structure that we set and follow restricting and cramping – but, to really be happy working on a show like these two, you need to embrace the restrictions and stretch yourself within the defined structure.

LEARN TO SAY WHAT YOU MEAN

Overwritten scripts are the bane of a television producer's life. There is nothing more frustrating to a deadline-pushed, budget-restricted producer than to have to wade through unnecessary scene description and elaborate stage directions that cloud the dialogue and characterisation of the vital story being told. In every case, I would ignore these anyway. Keep the scene description (or slugline) to the bare minimum. Set the scene. No more. No less.

Timing issues are also a thorn in a producer's side. Every script will be routinely timed at second draft and, if it is overrunning, the script editor will be instructed to make sure the next draft comes in on time. I for one used to get very frustrated with finding we had to cut scripts in the offline edit, meaning I had wasted time, and therefore money, getting the script shot only to find it wasn't to length and had to be cut.

A script may stretch in the filming, and this often happens if, for example, we are using an older actor who labours the dialogue more than someone younger. Character acting can also sometimes be the reason a script changes length. In the case of the fabulous June Brown and her *EastEnders* character Dot Cotton I would sit in the gallery watching her do a scene and know, without a doubt, that she had just cut two minutes off the overall length because she talked so fast. Fortunately for us, June was marvellous at ad-libbing and would fill out a scene if called for – but, again, this had its downside, as she was often rather hard to stop. Or sometimes the action sequences come out longer in the shooting than was allowed for at the production draft stage. So mistakes can happen and sometimes overrunning is unavoidable.

It is always better, in my view, to only say what you really need to on the page, and to write like you are running out of time. Get the important stuff into the script, and therefore in front of the camera, and leave out anything extraneous to plot, characterisation or visual impact.

PRACTISE BEING PITHY

Being succinct and clear in your outlines and treatments for the work you create is a really good exercise to get used to doing daily.

Pare down your scene descriptions and extraneous dialogue, and be exacting and specific with the imagery you use. If it is the right image, it will do the job of several.

TREATMENT WRITING

Love 'em or hate 'em, they are part and parcel of the writing experience for all committed, serious, trying-to-make-a-go-of-it writers. The reason they are so important is primarily because, unless you want to write scripts for yourself and maybe read them out after Christmas dinner around the turkey carcass, you will need to sell your idea to someone who can make it happen on screen for you, and this is a surefire way of getting your idea, your voice, your message, your talent and your craft across. Convinced? I hope so because this business of treatment writing will not go away and if you are, like a lot of writers, not the best at tackling them, here are my tips for writing better ones.

BE SUCCINCT

Brief, concise, pithy; sound bite, morsel, nugget – any way you cut it this treatment writing business is about getting to the point and sticking to it. Avoid at all costs superfluous description and rambling in general. In this document, you will be presenting your idea in as pared down a way as you can, distilling its essence and, by doing so, revealing the best bits and tempting the reader to want more. Less, in treatment writing like in so much else, is more.

BE VISUAL

Astonishing, I know, but very often I find myself reminding writers that we are working in a visual medium and that, by the very nature of what we do, we must be visual at all times. In a treatment, you are not only drawing in your reader (who may then become your buyer, your audience and ultimately your critic) with your use of words and ability to present a tempting tale; you are also encouraging them to visualise your story, characters and the world you have created in microcosm. So every image you present in the treatment must be the right one, the only one – the very best to do the job you have given it.

ENJOY THE ENGLISH LANGUAGE

Here's another odd revelation in regard to the craft of writing: some writers need to be reminded that we are in the business of communication. So enjoying, exploring and experimenting with your mother tongue and, in particular, the way you express yourself are key to getting your script right, and should therefore be central to writing the seminal treatment. Treatments are about description; they imagine, underline and highlight the best elements of your intended story, the best characterisation and the 'feel' of what you intend to develop in your script. So taking control and mastering the art of enticement by deft use of descriptive, romantic and arresting language will result in an open, alluring treatment that grips from the start.

BE ENTERTAINING

Commissioners and producers can be a jaded bunch – I speak not only from general, but also personal experience of this. So make it your business to get the attention of your reader in the first second of your treatment. It sounds obvious but, if your idea is a comedy, the way you present your world and your characters should at some stage raise a smile. If your idea is a medical drama, a crime format or a rom-com, the language will again need to reflect the genre. Entertain your reader by echoing the tone of the proposed drama in your treatment. We are in the business of communication, education, distraction and entertainment, so make your treatment sing in all of these areas.

THE GENERAL LAYOUT OF A TREATMENT

Title: Make yours really sell your idea by being the best you can make it. Favourite titles? *Call the Midwife. Roger and Val Have Just Got In.* Sometimes it's better that the title describes what's in the tin, so to speak – e.g. *Good Cop* or, to take an example of a show I produced for CITV, *My Dad's a Boring Nerd*.

Format description: I have covered already the series/serial definitions that I have used for 20 years in the industry, but, if this is not a long-running idea, state whether it's a two-, four-, or six-parter.

Logline: In no more than three or four lines, summarise your idea as entertainingly and as succinctly as you can. You need to convey the main narrative here – the set up, the jeopardy or challenge for your protagonist – and to give a sense of style and tone by the way you word this. It's hard to do, but essential.

One paragraph of tasty description setting out the world: Here the job is to be as descriptive and evocative as possible – imagine you are telling your friend about a film you have just seen that truely made an impact on you. You need to entice them into the storyline, to make them want to see it, too.

Character biographies: Make these as tasty as you can. I like to add a quotation relating to each character under their name; the sort of thing they are most likely to say or something that alludes to their particular storyline. For example, in a treatment I wrote, ostensibly about The Eternal Quest For Mr Right and entitled *A Man For All Seasons* (I did not ask the estate of Robert Bolt but, if it had been commissioned, I would have had to rethink this), I created a character called PLUM. Her quotation was 'Plum is looking for a man she can spar with; so far, she has only dated those that shop there.' In each character biog, give a suggestion of the arc of their storyline across the number of episodes, or across the span of the script you are intending to write. Make these people live on the page.

Episode outline: I think this is self-explanatory – but be exacting and succinct in your language whilst being as interesting as you can in the layout of your storyline. Give the thrust of the A (or main) storyline, with the smaller B and C stories, if you have them, running parallel.

Main story arcs: Each character has a journey and here you outline what that is in story terms. Again, pithy, evocative language is what we are looking for.

The central message: This will be alluded to in your logline at the top of the treatment, but here you can extrapolate a bit more and dig a bit deeper.

Throughout the writing of your treatment you must also pay attention to the style and tone of your writing and, as much as possible, evoke for your reader the flavour of what they will ultimately be seeing on screen.

STORYLINING

No one is saying that storylining is easy – or even interesting. It's not always; sometimes it's just a hard, plotting slog. But in the planning of any drama, be it a single or a series, an un-produced or production script, it is essential that your storylines are plotted properly.

Storylining is something writers should do in their sleep. Do it a lot.

It will get easier and with experience the obvious beats will slot themselves in place without you even noticing, leaving you to concentrate on digging out the beats in a storyline that are not so obvious, but which, once discovered, will make all the difference to the original idea.

Because, believe me, and I say this with a bleeding heart (having had to steer script-editing sessions well into the early hours after a storyline has been allowed to go walkabout during the drafting process and ended up infecting a bunch of scripts ready to go to camera), you will write too much, you will veer off the point, you will write yourself into a blind alley if you do not, firstly, work out the main and minor beats in the storyline and, secondly, work out how this storyline impacts and affects the other storylines in your script.

There are lots of reasons why, between creation and execution, a storyline can fall foul of the production process and ultimately end up a shadow of the original idea. It could be an issue of budget, episode length or actor availability, a compromise that has to be struck within the block of episodes through which your storyline is threaded, or a change of heart from the executive producer. But, regarding the execution of your storyline within your episode(s), if you stick to the storylining rule book, you won't go far wrong and you will find that your storylines naturally weave and loop around and through each other – thus giving your final script a real depth, a fitness, a resonance all of its own.

THE BASIC RULES OF STORYLINING

Know your length

Know the natural length of the storyline you want to create. Think about it instinctively and you will find that you land on a ballpark sort of length. Not all your storylines will need, or be able, to stretch the full length of the 25-minute, 60-minute or 90-minute drama you are writing. Some stories may be short and sweet and best plotted over perhaps only a third of your script; some may feature in the first two thirds and be resolved by the last 'act'. But every story has a natural length and you need to ascertain from the start what this is.

Know your rank

Decide if this storyline is an A or B or minor C storyline and plot it accordingly. An 'A' story is one that can best be described as 'what the episode is about' – it's the central theme, the message that forms the internal shape of your script/episode. A 'B' story takes up less script space but is important in that it will have the most impact on, and resonance with, the A story. A and B stories run parallel and interconnect throughout the script/episode, influencing the majority of the shape of the script. A 'C' story is a minor one, a smaller and shorter story, but still important in that it can undercut, contrast and conflict with, highlight or augment the A and B stories. In an average episode of *EastEnders* or *Emmerdale*, for example, there will be four or five storylines running concurrently with each other and right across the week's output. The idea is to get all stories, major and minor, doing a cohesive job together in each episode and also throughout the run of scripts produced.

Look for the detail

Once you've got the main beats in place – those moments where the drama literally peaks and the dramatic impact is most intensely felt – make sure you plot the lesser moments leading up to those dramatic highs. If you fail to carve out the detail of the quieter, subtler, gentler, subtextual moments in your storyline, the overall impact will be lessened and the pay-off you are looking for will not happen.

Work the connections

How do your storylines connect? How do they contrast with and highlight each other? Look at their separate paths: certain places where your storylines could interconnect and relate to each other will appear immediately obvious. However, there are also less obvious moments of interaction and reaction that are more difficult to identify.

How can each story get the best out of itself and the others in the script as a whole? There are crossover points in all stories and it is those junctions you will need to identify first.

Next, plot in the parallel moments of each storyline – when you allow your audience the opportunity to see and follow your separate stories and spend time with each one.

BE A STORY **CONTROL FREAK**

I cut my drama teeth on *EastEnders*. This fact made two things true about me:

- that I thrive on pressure
- that I like making stories happen

To continue in a symmetrical vein, this show also made me very good at two things in particular regarding the knotty problems we face when coming up with and constructing storylines, and I have regularly called upon these strengths in my career ever since:

- it made me fast at decision making
- it made me good at seeing the bigger picture

Whilst I'm not suggesting you become a swifter storyliner/creator/ writer, I *am* suggesting that you focus on getting an overview of your storylines; how they travel, not just across one hour of drama, but through a multi-part format.

Story Conferences expose you brilliantly to how stories are created and *EastEnders* has these every three months. It is like being at a marvellous story fair, where delegates sit around a table, and where story ideas, themes, concepts and character arcs are presented and discussed, dissected and ultimately distributed to the writers present. Writers come to pitch ideas, and also to listen to, and pitch in on, fellow writers' storylines. The executive producer has final say over what will ultimately be in the story document.

This is not the time in the writer's calender to be shy and retiring. You need to be strong in your opinions and have collaboration at the forefront of your thinking if you are going to be heard and taken seriously.

Writers who contribute to an already established series or serial need to be able to write great pitches and also sell them at the Story Conference.

The Story Conference process teaches you, almost subliminally, not only to recognise a great storyline, but also how to create and pitch them as you get more experienced at contributing and giving your input. Very quickly, you will find that you are able to pick out a storyline that has the potential to go more than a couple of episodes and recognise when a truly fabulous storyline presents itself – even if it is only the edge of one that you can see.

Experience teaches you that digging a bit deeper into that idea will reveal a wealth of other storylines that are off-shoots and tributaries of the initial storyline. So a small idea can often become a huge unwieldy beast that needs plotting over many episodes.

Here's an illustrative example about storylining. Tony Jordan (when writing regularly for *EastEnders*) came up with the storyline of Phil Mitchell's affair with his sister-in-law Sharon whilst Grant, his brother, was in prison for GBH. We knew this wasn't going to be a medium-sized storyline; their affair revealed so many facets of the personalities of the three characters involved, and the impact of their betrayal of Grant was felt by so many other characters in the square, that we found we could stretch that storyline to an inordinate length without losing its initial impetus. Grant had a history of violence, so that planted the seed of jeopardy into everything Phil and Sharon did, the audience naturally waiting with bated breath for him to find out, provoking a filial war in Walford.

We plotted this storyline across a whole year of the show's output. It ran and ran and ran. No one, not even Tony, had thought it had that much mileage, but that is the business of storylining; sometimes it's worth stretching an idea to the absolute limit to get everything out of it.

The episode that focused on Grant finding out, where Sharon and Phil had to face the music, got 22 million viewers.

A lot of writers I help now are unsure and lacking in confidence about storylining and making their stories go the distance of more than one episode. It seems to me that many writers do not have a problem structuring their stories across a traditional three-act single drama structure. Nor do they baulk when straying from this set format by writing more than three acts into their scripts. No, it is not the single format that seems to give writers the heebie jeebies; it is the two-, four- and six-parters, and (horror of horrors) the continuing drama formats, that cause the nervous breakdowns.

Take a break. Calmly does it. Here's how to think about longer-running formats.

CHARACTER JOURNEY

Each character you invent has a journey and a narrative path they must follow in order to earn their place in the first of your scripts. If your idea seems to fit into a format longer than a single, then it goes without saying that you are going to have to control their journey for longer.

And control it you must. Because there is nothing worse than a sloppily constructed storyline. A badly plotted, mismanaged storyline undermines the whole integrity of the script. Characterisation, dialogue, pace, emotional impact, the message and the tone are all directly affected. This might not be strictly the case if you are writing for an established series or soap, as the impact of the script before yours, and the one that comes after, will be felt by your episode, and so the symbiotic nature of this particular writing experience will stop you straying too far from the story document you write from. However, even within the rather more restricted format of a soap, the storyline will need bringing out, developing and weaving through your particular episode, and you need to control this.

In a more character-driven serial format like, for example, *The Syndicate* or *Last Tango in Halifax*, the craft of Kay Mellor and Sally

Wainwright respectively is clearly evident. Both these brilliant writers honed their skill working on series drama.

Get the storyline right, structure it right and you have the template you need to add all the other bells and whistles.

This sounds like a lot of work but it's important to do this stuff before you sit down and bash out your first draft of the first episode of your two-, four- or six-parter.

- **Identify the through-line of your storyline**
  What is the main thread that runs through it? What is it, essentially, about?

- **Plot the through-line in broad strokes across the number of episodes**
  Do this by using index cards, or sheets of paper, which you can rip up and move about, or use a whiteboard (I love a whiteboard, but you can get away with less overt expenditure!) I don't use a computer programme, but Scrivener is apparently useful, and also Final Draft has options to help you with storyline and structure. I find it useful to be visual, tactile almost, when plotting your storylines. Hemingway famously would peg his scenes on to a rope strung across his room. Do whatever works for you.

- **Identify the characters that your storyline most overtly affects**

- **Plot each character's through-line (their journey through the episodes) separately in broad strokes**

- **Plot each character's journey now in more detail**
  Make connections between each character's storyline, finding smaller and more emotionally resonant story beats.

- **Fill in the story gaps by making more connections and parallels for each character**
  Once you have pulled out your storylines in this way, you will be able to literally see where you can fill in any gaps that occur and where you may have missed a drama beat. The key to good storylining is to be both methodical and creative.

- **Plot the overview and then address the detail**

I would not leave anything to chance when you are writing an episodic drama. Get a system in place that works for you and stick to it when you embark on structuring your episodes.

Planting the seeds of a great storyline upfront, in the first ten pages of your first episode, and drawing the storyline out, carefully, with attention to both the broad and the more subtle story beats, will guarantee you have your audience still hooked by the end of your last episode.

When you storyline a multi-episodic drama well, you are taking the hand of your viewer and leading them through the duration of your drama – you don't leave them stranded at any point; you are in control of their experience the whole time.

Be the boss. Get good at structuring your storylines. Your work and your audience will thank you for it.

IT'S ALL ABOUT **THE STORY**

We hear this all the time. 'It's all about the script.' Well. It is.

But there are several key components to a well-crafted script: characterisation, dialogue, pacing, tone, visuals. And this stuff is not worth a kilojoule of writer effort without the Big One.

The story.

So let's put story first. Before all else. Story is the place where the drama starts.

And by 'story' I don't just mean what happens; what the sequence of events is in this tale. I don't just need to know how the action is triggered and, once under way, how the story, or narrative, plays out across your episode of television drama. Crucially, I need to know what the themes are that you seek to explore and what the message is that you want to convey, via both the text and the subtext of your story.

- **Plot/text:** the main action of your story; the engine that drives your script forward.

- **Subplot/subtext:** that which motivates character, affects, influences and adds to the main story across the episode.

- **Theme:** not the same as plot or text. Here I am talking about the ideas that your story throws up for inspection and consideration by your audience. So, for example, Sally Wainwright, in her series *Last Tango in Halifax*, shines a light on the sterling, surprising love of two pensioners and, in so doing, says a multitude of things about how we love today, how we observe older people, how the definition of family has changed over the decades since these two lovers were young, and how, in the final analysis, love really does conquer all.

- **Message:** so, after your story has been told, what is it you want to say to your audience? What is it that you would like your audience to take away with them after the credits roll?

The healthy future of television drama is dependent on two simple things being consistently true:

- that writers have strong opinions
- that, as creative individuals, their need to express those opinions and to have their stories told via the small screen is supported by their actual writing talent

Sadly, ability cannot be taught, but the craft of writing can. So let's get down to business. A story has a multi-layered job to do. A good story multi-tasks. Creating a story for television, the writer needs to be doing the following:

- **Expressing an opinion** – what is it you want to say and what is your point of view?

- **Engaging the audience** – does your story enable an audience to be drawn into the narrative?

- **Being relevant** – does the story resonate with your potential audience?

A story expresses and extracts opinion. It engages an audience by being relevant to their lives. In turn, the audience empathises with the story, shares it and, by extension, celebrates that story and the characters that tell it.

Make sure you have something to say and set your story stall out in such a way that as many people as possible want not only to hear your opinion, but also to form one of their own.

Having an opinion is, of course, not enough; we all have those. Neither is the need to communicate; that is, after all, human nature.

Telling a story well is what separates skilled writers from the shaggy-dog storyteller, the anecdote profferer, the person who builds a 60-page script around what turns out to be just a moment and not a full story.

For a story to work, you need text to marry subtext and have theme come to the wedding.

AND IT'S ALSO ALL ABOUT
THE STORYLINE

Imagine that you have been invited to attend a Story Conference for a long-running show on a big commercial channel. Does this fill you with an unnamed dread? Or do you have a rush of adrenalin considering the prospect? Whether your reaction is a gurn or a grin, I recommend you apply the process outlined in this chapter to your single screenplay storylines as well as your serialised ideas.

Obviously, the single screenplay does not require your storyline to have 'legs' or any prospect of continuing beyond the length you have written (a 60-minute or 90-minute television script). But, within the length of this single story, there will be more than one storyline, and each must have a cohesive journey across the length of the script; so you will need to storyline, control and orchestrate the path of each one.

The two-parter, e.g. *The 7.39* (BBC), the three-part drama, e.g. *In the Flesh* (BBC), the four-part serial, e.g. *Chasing Shadows* – a new (at the time of press) ITV commission – or the longer-run six-part serial, e.g. *Breathless* (ITV), demand close storylining, as do the multi-episode series like *Casualty*, or indeed our soaps, like *Corrie*, *EastEnders* or *Emmerdale*, which have no definable ending. Each storyline must be created from the outset with the potential to span more than one episode.

How do you do this?

The initial idea can come as a moment in the life of your character, but you must ensure that it is more than just a moment, an image, a suggestion of a story. You need to build on that beat and expand it to reach across more than one episode.

Many times, you will find that the idea you had for a story was just that: a moment in time that does not hold any power or longevity. It is not to be dismissed necessarily; it can form part of the overall arc of your storyline, but it is not a story in itself, merely a beat, a twist, a moment.

A real storyline has a purpose, a subtext, a drive and a message, and something or someone must be doing the driving.

The springboard moment, or the inciting incident, is the start point. The jumping-off point. The point at which, on reflection, looking back, your character can say, 'That was where it all started to change for me.'

The storyline that delivers good story is all about the journey, not the destination.

There is a hiatus, a moment of apparent calm and understanding, that you are aiming for now, in your storyline. But you need to muddy the waters first, as many times as you can get away with, in order to keep up and engage both the momentum of your narrative and the interest of your audience.

Plot twists. Television loves them. Dramatists understand that a linear storyline with a predictable outcome is the worst kind of dull for on-screen drama. So have your protagonist do an 180-degree turn and take them somewhere you know your audience will not expect.

Use other characters and their motivations to help send your main protagonist off on a tangent. The long-run format of series and soaps truly comes into its own when you can create connections, crossovers and counterpoints with other storylines and other character arcs.

The key to all good storylining lies in the ability to make these patterns, these story relationships.

Good storylining enables characters to step off into the unknown, poke about, get hurt, recoil, learn something, meet someone, find out something; all the while building to the moment of self-realisation or decision, of learning the truth, of accepting the inevitable, of coming to terms with their storyline and themselves.

Along the way, you need to deliver key dramatic moments an audience can latch on to, in order to further explain the plot line, or to reveal something essential about the characters.

Audiences remember dialogue – but tying these into a visual is the perfect way of getting your viewers to take the story home with them, so storylines have to be visual as well as articulated by dialogue and character.

A strong serial storyline has a buoyant story arc, personified and explored by a particular character or character grouping. In this way, the storyline is different from the rest of the episode, because it has a job to do that is particular to the character, or characters, it explores. But this storyline is also very much a part of the bigger picture, in that it has a symbiotic relationship with the other storylines in the episode as a whole. A good serial storyline affects and influences other characters, and therefore other storylines, throughout the episode.

EXAMPLE OF THE SHORT-DISTANCE STORYLINE

Character X meets a blast from the past. Initially, it is lovely to catch up, but she learns more than she wants to about his life over the past decade and decides not to rekindle the flame.
Suggested length – 2–3 episodes.

EXAMPLE OF THE LONGER-DISTANCE STORYLINE

Character X is always broke. He decides to put a month's wages on one lottery ticket. He doesn't win. Fighting drunk, he hits rock bottom. Depressed, he seeks help and starts the road to recovery.
Suggested length – 3–4 episodes.

EXAMPLE OF THE FULL-DISTANCE STORYLINE

Character X's child goes missing. She becomes the prime suspect in his disappearance. This storyline can run for as long as your series dictates. There is so much to be explored here; this is the sort of storyline that producers use to arc across whole series' output. The beats are numerous, there are many different directions this storyline could take and the impact will be felt to a greater or lesser extent by the other characters in the series. It is the sort of emotive subject matter that engenders strong reactions and opinion.

THE STORYLINE DOCUMENT

Once you have pitched, discussed, argued, defended, admitted defeat or been victorious in having your storyline accepted, the storyliners get busy.

They will produce a document not dissimilar to the one below.

This storyline document pertains to a fictitious series called *Harkness Hall* that I created and wrote to form the blueprint for my 'How to Storyline for Television' workshops.

Harkness Hall exists only in the minds of as many writers as I can get to across the country; it is an exercise, not a commissioned show; the following content, characters and locations are my copyright.

I outline here how to use the document and how to map out and present your storylines, which comprise the A, B and C stories that fit into each episode of any given block of episodes in a long-running series.

This is the sort of template I have used on *Crossroads* and *Holby City*. The way these documents are laid out changes, but their purpose is the same.

HARKNESS HALL: STORYLINE DOCUMENT

Episode Number:
TX:
CAST (tick if featured)
LADY SKYE HARKNESS
LORD JONATHON HARKNESS
ROWAN HARKNESS

CHARLIE HARKNESS
CHARLOTTE HARKNESS
ANNIE LEEVES
MATTHEW STEVENS
GABRIEL SUMMERS
LILY SUMMERS
BEATRICE MATLOCK
MARK MATLOCK
TOM DAVIES
JASMINE HARPER
SHELLY HARPER
PETE
SIMON
RUDY

SETS (tick if featured)
INTERIORS:

HARKNESS HALL
THE KITCHEN
THE CONSERVATORY
THE STUDY
SKYE AND JONATHON'S BEDROOM

HOME FARM
THE SITTING ROOM
BEATRICE'S BEDROOM
MARK'S BEDROOM

THE PLOUGH INN
THE BAR

TOM'S VET SURGERY

JASMINE/SHELLY'S HOUSE

THE MILL – RUDY'S STUDIO

EXTERIORS:

THE GROUNDS
THE LILAC WALKWAY
THE WALLED VEG GARDEN
OAKWOOD

HOME FARM
FARMYARD/FIELD/THE LANE

THE PLOUGH INN
SEATED AREA AND GARDEN

HARKNESS HALL
BLOCK ONE: TX: JUNE 2014

EXEC PROD: **SCRIPT EDITORS:**
PROD: **STORYLINERS:**
STORY EXEC:

THE 'A' STORY:
TITLE/CHARACTER(S)/GROUPINGS/LOCATION/SET
Put the names of the characters that carry, and are pertinent to, the 'A' storyline you have in this particular episode and the location in which it takes place, e.g. SKYE/ANNIE/ROWAN – INT: HARKNESS HALL

Pick-up cliff: (insert logline)
Outline here, in a few lines only, the arc of the 'A' story as it begins and ends in this episode. This is so the writer can see at a glance what the pick-up point of the story is and where it ends, so it can be picked up by the next episode.

Now write the storyline as it was plotted at the Story Conference. Use roughly a paragraph per scene. There should be approximately 5–6 paragraphs to this story.

Within each paragraph (or scene) you need to mark the steps, or drama beats, along the storyline as it appears in this episode. Each episode in the block will be focusing on a further step along the storyline that was plotted on the board at Story Conference.

As both storyliner and writer, you can decide, once the story document is written, how you choose to structure the scenes across your episode. This document is meant to show clearly the drama beats of the storylines that have been created.

Write the story with a descriptive flair. Describe how your characters interact and feel in a prose style, describing what is said and done, but do not use dialogue as this comes later, when the first draft is written from this document.

Cliffhanger moment: (insert two pithy lines to end your episode)

THE 'B' STORY:
TITLE/CHARACTER(S)/GROUPINGS/LOCATION/SET
Pick-up cliff: (insert logline)

As per conference, write up your 'B' story. Be descriptive, but succinct. These paragraphs should entice you, the writer, to want to write the scenes you outline here. Allow approximately 3–4 paragraphs for this slightly smaller storyline.

Cliffhanger moment:

There may be more than one story classed as a 'B' in a typical long-form drama episode.

THE 'C' STORY:
TITLE/CHARACTER(S)/GROUPINGS/LOCATION/SET
Pick-up cliff: This may not have a pick up point, but be created just for this episode. This is often a more comedic story, designed to lighten the drama tone throughout the episode.

The storylines are now in place and the scripting process can begin.

THE RELATIONSHIP WITH YOUR **SCRIPT EDITOR**

A good script editor (and I sincerely hope you only work with good ones) will not only be able to improve your script with confidence, but will also make the process enjoyable and even stimulating.

A fantastic script editor, the best (the sort, of course, that I hope I managed to morph into over the years that I did the job), will not only make your work better and give you a very pleasurable experience; after the final draft has been delivered and your baby is twinkling away under the studio lights on the day of principal recording, you will probably not be able to recall how it was that you changed your original plot twist to this much better one in Sc 20, or the process that resulted in the marvellous cliffhanger that so seamlessly bleeds into those iconic drum beats as the famous signature tune kicks in.

But a process was most definitely followed and your script editor was taking you through it, draft by crafted draft. It was done with humour, some delicacy and a lot of solid common sense.

A good, expert, fantastic script editor will be able to give you script notes (some large, some small, some irritating, some illuminating) without you, the writer, ever feeling exposed, or unsure, or feeling that your work is being ridiculed, overly criticised or downright changed too much.

The writer on any long-running show is an essential part of the dramatic process because, obviously, without them there wouldn't be a script. However, although they are very important, it is in fact the writer's relationship with the script editor that is – on the long-distance, story-gobbling, writer-exhausting, fast-running train that is the drama series format – in many ways, more critical.

The key to a good relationship with your script editor is collaboration and an ability on your own part to let go a bit.

The editor assigned to your script has a job to do which involves several layers; it is a complicated and demanding job, but its main element is to deliver your script to camera, to length, with all the correct story beats, character development and plot lines intact, with the correct amount of ad breaks and a fabulous cliffhanger, to deadline. If you don't invest in the relationship between your script editor and yourself, if you find it hard to take notes and instead make the process an uneasy, unenjoyable one, it all falls apart quickly and it's then that much harder for everyone to get the script you are writing to camera on time.

The script editor sits in the sometimes rather turbulent waters between the writer and the show's producer. It is their job to pass on all the producer's concerns and notes on your draft to you, without drawing any blood or, hopefully, generating any tears.

Script editing is a job that demands innovation and a creative brain. A good editor will be able to infuse more drama into your script, give you suggestions of better or more numerous plot twists, direct you into more interesting territory via a character or group of characters, and generally enthuse you into doing a better draft at each session. It's also a collating, organising, structuring job. According to the rigours of a particular show, there will be so many sets allowed, so many locations, and in every block of scripts there will be a certain number of characters that must be catered for in story terms. There'll be a story document into which the script editor may or may not have had any input, and you will both use this to keep to the correct plot line and deliver the correct drama beats so that your script will pick up and hand over the storyline at the right point. It's a job that demands the juggling of both creative and administrative information.

So they work hard, these script editors. And they often do so behind the scenes, as it were. The writer (quite rightly so) gets the credit for the marvellous script and hopefully continues to get commissioned as part of the writing team, and the script editor gets to do it all over again with the next block of scripts.

Look out for the script editor as the credits roll. And make contact with them. They've certainly earned their place and can help you earn yours.

DEVELOPMENT:
EMBRACING THE ZEITGEIST

Zeitgeist. That word comes up a lot in television development circles. Everyone loves a project that hits it. Or is a step (not a leap – that would be too much too soon) ahead of it.

Meaning *the spirit of the times*, it sums up for me what television drama development is all about.

I know that writers often worry about not being original when they discover the horrible truth about a fabulous idea they had whilst squeezing a tea bag with the back of a spoon: that this idea of theirs has not only been thought of by someone else, but has actually been made already and is transmitting on BBC2.

However, the fact that you share great ideas with Matthew Graham or Rae Earl, I would say in response, is a good thing. They had the obvious clout to make it happen, or else they got their big break whilst yours is still a way away, but be assured that all is well. You are hitting the Zeitgeist along with some of the best writers on television.

Now you just have to get really good, really quickly, so that you, in a few years' time, can be doing just that: snatching the most engaging, commercially appealing, creatively stretching ideas out of the ether and getting your stories told, while the newbies on the block collectively cry out that they are not original enough, or well known enough.

Another tricky area that often gets discussed on forums and the like, when writers are engaged in development of their project with other parties, is copyright.

A BIT ABOUT COPYRIGHT

The simple truth to remember here is that no one, not even that mysterious gardener who planted the first seed of the original drama tree, can copyright an idea. We all have them, all of the time; ideas are in the public domain. But you can and should copyright your execution, development and depiction of that idea in script form.

However, remember that if you take a one-page pitch, or a six-page treatment, or a slip of paper with a cracking logline on it, or a whole 120-page feature-length script to a drama development person, you will have started a paper trail that leads back to your project.

From the first email you send, with the title in the subject bar, to the final contract you (happily) sign, there is a physical, readable, tangible path leading from the project in question back to you.

You can protect your words, your characters, your execution of an idea simply by naming and dating your script pages, adding the copyright symbol and posting the work to yourself.

The Writers' Guild of Great Britain Association (WGGA) has a helpful website covering this issue and others relating to writing: *http://www.writersguild.org.uk/faqs/24-how-do-i-copyright-my-script-and-please-can-i-have-some-information-about-copyright-*

The copyright laws in the US are different from those in the UK, so if you are sending work abroad, or are involved in a development project across the pond, I would recommend you access the Writers' Guild Association East website, which shows you how to register your work and what the costs are: *https://www.wgaeast.org/script_registra tion/?gclid=CMPO8tO4srwCFfLHtAodNOYAQg&cookie_check=1*

WORKING WITH OTHERS

If you are collaborating with another writer, discuss before you get involved in any creative process how you want to proceed. Draw up a simple contract (a verbal one is not enough, should matters become confused later, as to ownership, so written is always best). This is to make sure both of you are aware of, and agree with, the input you expect from the other.

Often, the writing of the treatment for the drama idea irons out such areas as creative input. If both of you came up with the idea together, then, once you have the title and the beginnings of a treatment, you will be able to write under that title 'Created and developed by X and X'. Or, if you brought the idea to the table but want a writer to co-write the idea with you, the treatment might say something like 'Created by X and written in collaboration with X'. The wording must reflect the actual truth about your writing relationship.

The way you work creatively is also important to iron out early on. There will be several pertinent questions you need to ask yourselves before you get down to the good stuff:

Are you both early birds, or do you find the ideas don't flow before 11 am?

Do you like lots of little breaks, or are you more likely to crash on through till lunch time?

Do you even write in the same room? Is it better for both of you if this collaboration is conducted entirely online or via Skype?

Who does the scribing, and who does the talking? Some writers like to walk around the room, talking, whilst their partner makes quick notes, to recap later. Or both members of the team will sit at computers and fly comments across the desktop to each other as they amend their documents on screen.

If there is a note taker in your midst, is this role interchangeable?

If there are disagreements (and, of course, there will be) how are you going to resolve them?

Work out your modus operandi early on, and then you can let the fun begin.

Development is all about collaboration and the push and pull of creative minds working together. Pairings can be very fruitful if the right match is made from the off. Sam Bain and Jesse Armstrong are television's superhero writer collaborators. Their joint CV reads like a *Who's Who* of television, and their list of credits shows a glittering array of big-hitting winners in the comedy genre: *Smack the Pony*, *My Parents Are Aliens*, *Peep Show* and *Fresh Meat*, to name a few.

More unusually, but often just as potently, writer teams can be composed of family members. The dynamic duo Bryan Elsley and his son Jamie Brittain are testimony to how a healthy collaboration can really produce the goods. Their series *Skins* is a case in point.

Writing does not have to be a solo activity and writing in a partnership, although not for everyone, can be a very happy experience for those concerned.

Here I talk to Jeff Povey about the process he, the irrepressible Tony Jordan and their fellow writers followed when coming up with the BBC television drama series *By Any Means*, produced by Tony's company, Red Planet Pictures.

Jeff elucidates brilliantly that tricky balancing act between retaining your individuality as a creative thinker and ensuring that the writing partnership remains intact.

JEFF POVEY ON THE CREATION PROCESS

The collaboration was a Tony Jordan brainwave. He flew four writers out to Spain for a few days of intense blue-sky thinking. We weren't to prepare beforehand and all ideas were to be on the spot, dragged kicking and screaming from the creative collective.

A judge or invigilator came along with a notebook. This notebook could only be written in if we unanimously agreed on an idea. The idea would go down on the page and we would congratulate ourselves, have a drink, then start again.

This sounds amicable and for the most part it was, but there is always the question of taste and tone. I didn't 'get' 90 per cent of the touted ideas and would never have wanted to go near them if they came to fruition. I think we all felt that way and keeping everyone happy and proactive was therefore a tricky balancing act. Hence the notebook and the need for universal agreement. It made you feel like you had contributed and had a certain ownership of an idea.

Luckily we were all mates, and had been for years, so we knew where someone might be taking a thought, and also how to jump all over it without resorting to pistols at dawn. That is probably an essential ingredient in the success of something like this. It can hurt but it's never personal. Well. Almost never.

I have always worked alone and the creation of an idea can take months, if not years, before you fully believe in it. This three-day brainstorm didn't suit my usual approach and, at times, I was reluctant to give even half an idea because my instinct would be to lock it away and nurture it. Sharing is difficult when you know that a great idea is GOLD in this business.

But I threw some thoughts out there and they were either shot down or we ran with them. Which was exciting. Having four brains taking a pitch in new directions, or just showing you that it didn't work, was both exhilarating and time saving. It also helped us understand each other better.

What we separately believed made good drama had to be merged somehow into one 'unimind' and, again, there were disagreements. My taste is nothing like anyone else's and I certainly don't think like anyone else, so holding on to your individuality in a collaboration is the hardest thing to do. You want to be you, but you also want to make the partnership work. It can't be a battle of wills and egos, either. It has to be a pure meeting of minds or it won't be a collaboration. This isn't easy when you've spent 20 years doing very well for yourself and, suddenly, everything that works for you has to be subsumed for the greater good.

To this end, I enjoy collaboration, but only up to a point. We emerged with an idea that the BBC commissioned and broadcast, and that was exhilarating; it proved that working with others can achieve a huge amount. But I am at heart my own man and, ultimately, it wasn't quite how I had envisaged the series.

At the end of the day you can only do things your way, and Tony had his take on it and he led the way. So, for me, it still comes down to the individual. We couldn't all have been in the room writing the first script. That would have really pushed the limits of our friendship.

WORKING WITH A SCRIPT EDITOR/DEVELOPMENT EXECUTIVE

They operate under different titles, but their job is the same. I have outlined this role in the industry paradigm earlier, so suffice it to say here that the person in question will have a slightly different agenda to you, but the process should be a happy one and the outcome positive, whether you end up with a fully fledged project, optioned and commissioned and script fee paid, or just a series of interesting meetings, resulting in a warm handshake and a 'Keep me informed of what you are up to'.

Bear in mind that the development executive will be keen to get as much mileage as possible out of you and your idea, whilst paying the going rate – no more, no less – for the work produced. You are in this to get as much development help and professional support and guidance as you can whilst working your socks off and hopefully having a good time in the process.

FROM TREATMENT, TO OUTLINE, TO SCRIPT

The overall structure of the development process within a television company openly foraging for ideas to develop further will depend on what it is you actually bring to the table at the first meeting.

If you are bringing a one-page pitch, or a couple of pages representing the idea in embryo, then the chances are you will be asked to develop it further, usually into a full **Treatment** (these can run from four to ten pages, depending on the nature of the beast).

This is work that is considered essential in television developmental circles if a project is to be taken seriously. It does mean that you are writing a pretty detailed, somewhat difficult document, with no financial incentive or guarantee that it will be taken further. But that is the way of the speculative development world.

The process of developing your idea from a couple of pages to a full-blown treatment can take anything from a couple of months to a year and beyond. And, still, the script that is begging to be written may not be commissioned at the end of this because there are more hurdles to jump first.

Once you have written the treatment and have a dynamite document that presents and explores your idea in perfect, succinct, arresting form, there will be a lull in proceedings whilst your new-found ally, the development executive, pushes forward the fledgling idea that you have been discussing, presenting their producer/executive with your treatment at their developmental meeting.

There will be a series of development meetings in place within a company keen to grow new dramas for their slate, and these can be held as regularly or as sporadically as is deemed fit for the outfit in question.

Here, producers will read and assess the projects on offer. Notes will be given, opinions formed, and your project may be kept in a holding pattern, with no decision being made at the current time, or given the green light and an option taken out on your treatment.

Often, projects that have not had the full support of the production executive will fall by the wayside here, and even those that are currently under option may find this is where the end of the line comes for them. It is at these meetings that all projects with options coming up for renewal will be considered, and the decision made whether to renew (thereby giving the company longer to develop the project) or not.

Projects that do not have their options renewed are now free to be taken elsewhere by your agent. A good one will already have ideas as to where the next potential interested party lies.

If, on the other hand, the development executive (whose instincts have clearly been right from the start) offers you an option on the treatment, this will essentially mean that you are now seeing some money for your efforts, and that, from now on, you are under contract to the company to develop your idea in collaboration with the development executive as they essentially see fit.

The option can run for only three months, but it is more usual to see options covering six or twelve or eighteen months. The fee offered is usually in the ballpark of £1,000, but some treatments may garner a little more and creep up to the £2,000 mark. Again, it depends on your track record as a writer with the company and within the industry in general, and also the size of the development budget at the disposal of the script person you are dealing with.

A word to the wise: there is a reason why the phrase 'development hell' is often heard in television drama circles. It is hell to wait, to not be in control of what happens to your squeakily exciting, Zeitgeist-punching idea. You have created this thing, this entity that you really believe in; it's got a great storyline and you are proud of the characters. But it's not your call any more. It's theirs. So get on their side and be positive about the reaction your project gets, albeit shining or a bit cloudy. The hurdle you jumped when you first got through the door of the development executive's office is behind you, and you have cleared the option hurdle, too.

Keep up the momentum now. Be accessible and open to new ways of looking at your idea; the world you created. The person who pushed for your idea to be accepted on to the development slate is now your champion. The next hurdle is in sight.

Producers need to know if your treatment for your series/serial has enough narrative force to cover more than a couple of episodes. This is the stage where you will most likely be asked to write a **Series Outline**.

Often, in an extended treatment which is under option, you will have been asked to provide a suggestion within it of where the series would go beyond the first couple of episodes. If you have done this already in some detail in the treatment then producers may not need to see more proof that the series you propose has 'legs'. However, more work may need to be done by you at this stage if the treatment lacks the longevity element.

I have covered outlines in an earlier chapter, so here I will say that it is at this point that you, the writer, are charged with making each episode subsequent to the first one you focused on in the treatment sound exciting, watchable and entertaining. Do not go through each story beat by beat; it may not be the case on screen, but this stuff makes for a laborious read. Make strong, sweeping, arching statements and keep your storylines moving through the episodes.

I have worked with writers who are happy to provide detailed storylines following on from the rough outline proposed in their treatment, so no more money exchanges hands at this juncture. However, occasionally I have been in the position where a writer's agent insists on a separate payment being made for the outline and, in this case, fees are again negotiated between the executive and the agent via the development executive.

It doesn't help any writer to be too pushy regarding payments for work done between treatment and script, and it is up to the producer whether an extra payment is made to cover the creation of a detailed outline. And, from the development executive's point of view, and that of their producer, it makes little sense to insist on too much work being done over too long a period without payment.

As with all things in life, a balance has to be drawn and agreed between all parties.

When you get to the final hurdle, you may be many months down the road from the days of your initial treatment, but now you have to produce the goods. The **Script Commission** is that shiny state you have been aiming for throughout the development process. This is where the executive and your (by now) Angel of Mercy, i.e. your development executive, decide, via one of those development meetings, to go to script. Fees vary, depending on the experience of the writer in question, their bankability and the nature of the project in question. This is where your agent comes into their own and obtains for you the best deal possible. All credits, rights, repeats, episodic credits and delivery dates are ironed out at this stage.

You now need to be free to focus on the job in hand. You need to write your first episode.

WORKING WITH **DOCUMENTS**

Writing for television isn't just about the creative process of writing good drama and all that this entails; it's also about being able to sell successfully not only your ideas, but also yourself as the catalyst for those ideas. Like a journalist, a television writer needs to be good at, or at the very least to get better at, precis, sound bites and pithy, arresting, succinct description, and to be able to speak, as well as write, in this style when pitching anything from a storyline up to a full treatment for a drama.

Being able to lay out in an easily digestible, attractive fashion an idea for a single, serial or series drama is a very good skill to have when writing for television. Producers love a tightly packaged, immediately accessible dramatic idea and the better you can make the 'selling' elements of this drama, the better it is for all concerned.

Producers need to know: what is the plot, where's the jeopardy, what is the theme, the central message, the tone, the style? Is it like something they can already picture? What were your influences? Then the practical stuff: what channel, what time slot, your key demographic and does it fit the bill? Of course, there are other considerations occupying the minds of commissioners and producers, but I mention the ones a writer should be able to engage with here.

These questions should be the key factors shaping your pitch document and treatment.

THE PITCH DOCUMENT

This should be a page at most, both for yourself, to clarify your thoughts, and for when you pitch it (if you intend this to be read by a producer or commissioner at a later date). The document should be a paragraph only, if you intend to pitch it verbally at a story meeting. It's a good idea to write a page and then reduce it down to an essential few lines that sum up the idea.

Your pitch document should contain:

- the setting (the world)
- the period (time)
- the essential turning point of your plot (the jeopardy, or what happens when)
- the protagonist or ensemble (key characters)

In the verbal pitch, you are essentially selling your story by showing its content and shape in as entertaining and interesting a fashion as possible in a very short space of time. The pitch document does the same job, but you have a page to do this.

THE TREATMENT

I have covered treatment writing already, but here I will add that it is an essential story document that television relies on in the initial stages of script development to hone the idea, to solidify any questions raised by the pitch document (when the idea was in embryo), and for you, the writer, to really nail all aspects of the story you have created. Treatments change as the idea grows – it's an organic story document but at some stage there will be a point reached where you and the producers believe it is time to write the outline.

THE OUTLINE – OR SCENE BY SCENE

Writing the outline will do several things for you. The first and the best benefit, in my view, is that it will force you to literally plot and confirm for yourself the drama beats of each plot line and character arc. It will also highlight any weaknesses in the mechanics of the storyline and expose any loose ends and character development issues. In writing the outline you are committing to your idea and wrestling with the nuts and bolts of the narrative. It is not necessary to write each scene in detail, but it is essential that you precis the content and intention of each scene as you go through your script, so you and the producer can see at a glance what is happening, where, and to whom. Outlining your script will also enable you to see the shape of your story and where plot lines could overlap, where scenes are best placed for maximum effect, and where there may be a hook, turning point or climax missing.

THE STORYLINE DOCUMENT

See the example of one earlier on page 60.

Being economical with language in the writing of treatments and pitches is great practice for when you are expected to work from a storyline document. The layout of this differs according to the show you are working on, but all long-running dramas have them and most of the serial formats, too. The style of writing in a storyline document is often pared down and journalistic in style. These are usually put together by the storyliners and/or the story editor. The job of this crucial document is to plot and trace the ongoing machinations of the various plot lines in each episode of a particular block, which are usually grouped together according to character groupings or families and categorised into A, B or C storylines (denoting the importance of the storyline and the weight it carries in that particular episode).

The storyliner will have boiled down the main plot beats of the A, B and C storylines in the episode you are writing to a series of paragraphs. To help you, they will have written a logline summary of the overall episode, and given you the in point and exit point of each storyline so the episode after yours links seamlessly. Your job is to interpret this document creatively whilst paying close attention to the mechanics of the document; keeping intact the in point, the out point and the various peaks in your featured storylines.

STRUCTURE

Writing is essentially about structure: how you choose to tell the story of the characters you have created and in what shape you decide to do this. By choosing your structure, you are determining the experience that, firstly, your script editor, producer and commissioner will have on reading your script, and, secondly and most importantly, the experience your audience will have whilst watching the completed episode on the screen. It is imperative that you get your structure right and the best television writers are exemplary at this part of the writing craft. Russell T Davies, Paul Abbott, Kay Mellor, Sally Wainwright, Jonathan Harvey and Matthew Graham are all from a series television background, having learned their craft on long-runners like *Coronation Street* and *EastEnders*. It is by writing shows like this that writers pick up, almost by osmosis, the business of structure and plotting storylines.

It is worth noting here that television writers often expand on the traditional three-act structure for their episodes. The first act, if you are writing for a commercial channel, will be followed by an ad break. The second act is often split into three (i.e. acts two, three and four, followed by an ad break), and the final act, the fifth, will segue into the last commercial break and next programme, marking the end of the episode. So it is not unusual to come across television drama scripts with four or five acts. It all depends on the requirements of the channel.

DIALOGUE

Television writing is as near to theatre as you can get without a proscenium. A visual medium, yes, but at its base root it is dialogue-led. This brings in very quickly the need to be able to create character and write engaging, shaped dialogue that explores the text and develops the subtext in each scene. Great dialogue comes from a grounded, realistic root and is always born out of believable, three-dimensional characters. The writers listed above are all obviously extremely talented in this area, but if you take particular notice of any writing on screen it will, in the main, be because you like the dialogue.

HOOKS

The clue is in the name – what is it in the story that snags the attention of the reader or viewer? How do you grab and keep their attention? A hook can be a lead hook, which is an introduction into a scene or sequence of scenes; a narrative hook, i.e. a key moment when the plot turns or twists; or a visual hook, without dialogue, where what they see on screen rivets the viewer and carries their attention into the next scene. How do you keep your reader turning the pages and your viewer from using the remote and changing channels? Hooks are vital and should be plentiful in a television script. Plant your hooks carefully; they won't all be big moments, but should vary in size and intensity. Their presence in a script makes it sing.

CLIFFS

Visual again. Leaving the episode hanging on a line, a moment, a look or a piece of action is the cliffhanger of the script. How you get out of the episode determines the shape and intensity of your cliff.

MISTAKES TELEVISION WRITERS MAKE

Believing you, the writer, are bigger than the sum of the show's parts.
If you are part of a writing team on a series or serial, you are an essential but expendable element of the scripting process. The script is essential but the writer of that script is not. Without the script, there is no drama, but a budget- and time-strapped producer can and will make the changes necessary to get the script camera ready within the time and budget restrictions.

Viewing your script edit sessions as a potential battleground.
Your script edits with your script editor should be mutually respectful areas of time in the scripting schedule where you have the right to contest notes given but do not have the ultimate sign-off on any decision.

Hiding behind your agent.
Everyone needs a solid professional to fight their corner should a problem with contract, fee, delivery dates, or a personal issue arise during your commission period on a TV show. But be visible and approachable during these times as the production team want to feel their show has a champion in you, not an adversary.

Straying too far off the script document pertaining to your script.
On most long-running shows, the script document has been painstakingly produced via a series of Story Conferences and meetings with the producer and the script team. It is the skeleton, the blueprint

and the reference document that the production follows to keep the episodes coherent and cohesive. Keeping to the brief this sets out when writing your script ensures an easy and enjoyable writing experience on the show.

Being a slave to the script document.

It sounds unfair, I know, but this is another mistake that is often made, to the detriment of the writer's time on the show and to the show in general. A slavish adherence to the drama beats outlined by the storyliners in your script document will make a rather dull and predictable episode. The producer hired you for your voice – so do, please, use it!

Bringing the party to the table.

Believe it or not, there's many a series Story Conference that has been ruined by too much fun and games during the lunch breaks. Keep a sober and level head – even, as the adage goes, when those about you are losing theirs.

Not listening to fellow writers.

Story Conferences are sometimes rather political elements of the story production process. An oft-made mistake is when writers (maybe through their own enthusiasm and keenness to impress) do not listen or take on board the input of their colleagues when discussing storylines.

Consistently missing deadlines.

It's hard, being expected time and again to deliver to a time deadline. But on a long-running drama series it is essential that the script arrives when the schedule demands and, if you consistently miss this date, it puts huge pressure on every member of the production team. Some savvy script editors will add a bit of 'wiggle room' into your delivery schedule, therefore giving themselves a slight contingency if things go pear-shaped for any reason. Even if you have breathing room, do not abuse it.

Once you've delivered, then you are done.

On a series, this is often not the case. On a show like *EastEnders*, for example, you will be expected to be available for notes, and for consultation with a member of the script team about your script, right up to the point of shooting, and in some cases be expected to attend the actual day's shoot. If you do attend the shoot, you will be paid an attendance fee.

Giving storylines away.

An absolute no-no, but sometimes this still happens. From time to time, the production might welcome a leak, for publicity purposes, but, in the main, the writer should most definitely leave any story giveaways to the publicity department.

WRITING **UNDER COMMISSION**

Well done. You've managed to get to the final hurdle in the race to become a professional writer (i.e. one who is paid to write). Once you are over this and have signed on the dotted line to deliver a script as part of a series or serial for television, a whole new vista will open up before you.

Now you are part of the team. No longer do you run solo. No more tripping up, falling over and scraping your knees. This time, now, you have to perform to the very best of your ability and show your peers just what a natural athlete you are.

A producer has signed a writers' contract dictating that you deliver an episode of their particular series, or serial, on a certain date. The contract will state that you must deliver the first draft on a particular date, as well as writing subsequent drafts in accordance with the stipulations of the show and guided with regard to deadlines by a named script editor.

The contract will also state the final draft delivery date, which will be calculated from the date of expected TX (or transmission) of your episode. The timeline will be approximately six weeks from the date of contract signature to final draft delivery.

Writing on a fast-turnaround show like *EastEnders*, *Coronation Street* or *Emmerdale*, writers will be expected to deliver their first draft within two weeks of the signing of the contract and to keep up momentum on delivery until their final draft is delivered to the production office.

I have worked on soaps that have been strapped across the week, by which I mean transmitting an episode every day, five days a week.

This is truly gruelling for everyone concerned. However, it is amazing how fast and effective writers, production teams, directors and actors can become with practice and a transmission deadline approaching. There is nothing in this world more terrifying to a producer than the threat of a blank television screen.

On shows of this magnitude, there is no time or room in the schedule for more than three drafts maximum before the episode must be at shooting script stage. In this scenario, writers have to be really instinctive about story and confident about their ability to deliver. The script teams have to work to a strict schedule and the whole process becomes akin to a script-producing factory.

Transmitting four episodes a week with an omnibus repeat, *EastEnders* is approaching a similarly frenetic production schedule. This show, however, still allows for four or five drafts per episode.

I outline below a five-draft scenario: three drafts plus rehearsal and shooting script stages, bringing the full total to five drafts of one script.

The various drafts are colour-coded to ensure the script team know at a glance which stage of writing any particular script is at, at any one time.

The colours may vary from show to show, but this is how they looked on the shows I script edited and produced.

FIRST DRAFT – BLUE

The main body of notes is given at this stage, between first and second draft. Your script editor will be covering lots of different areas of your script in order to get the best results from you, in the shortest time. He or she will have had their meeting with the producer; your script has therefore already gone through one rigorous filter system and now the script editor must pass on these notes to you, in a clear, supportive way, and also add their own notes/concerns regarding your first draft episode.

There will be practical issues to address here: have you used the correct sets and followed the location to interior set allocation? Are there any cast issues that need to be passed on to you? (Sometimes actors become unavailable during the scripting process, which is always a bind as whole or parts of storylines must be altered, either to fit a reduced shooting schedule or replace a cast member entirely from a particular block of episodes.)

And there will be some homework to do: have you followed your given storyline? Are there any continuity issues arising from the way you have explored your particular storyline? Sometimes, when a storyline has more than one obvious peak, or high point, within it, writers are at risk of repeating the same, or a similar, dramatic moment between the same characters. Ringing the dramatic changes between each episode and making sure all drama beats are covered is a fundamental first draft note from your script editor.

A slavish adherence to the storyline document, with no added light or shade from you, will result in a dull episode. The script editor will be looking for those moments that you brought to the table: those lovely character touches; the added texture, levity or moments of pathos that you have fashioned into your episode. They will want to see that you have made it your own.

Timing is always an issue on a fast-turnaround show, so there will be a nod towards this in your first draft edit session. Extraneous dialogue, exposition, ugly, clunking exchanges, pages with too much blocky text and not enough action will be cut, trimmed and reshaped. The script editor will (with your collaboration) bring the overall length of the script down, trimming off the flabby bits and getting the script into a leaner shape for the second draft.

SECOND DRAFT – PINK

Now a cleaner, clearer draft. If you have had to do any serious re-storylining, any continuity or narrative issues are sorted out at this stage. There are three advertising breaks for ITV programmes, so writers tend to write in four acts, not the traditional three-act structure, and it is at this draft stage that any niggling structural problems will need to be addressed and sorted for the next draft. The length will be looking more within the ballpark now. If your tendency is to underwrite, here the script editor will be helping you beef up dramatic moments, add more texture, develop a subtextual storyline more, or suggest ways you can increase pace or action.

THIRD DRAFT – GREEN

The final polish before your script becomes a rehearsal script. The director will most likely need to give you notes at this stage and, working with your script editor, you will go through the episode from his/her point of view. After changes, the script will be passed to the director's PA and distributed to the cast, and made available to all the heads of department and the production team.

REHEARSAL SCRIPT – WHITE

Once here, you will be making changes, via your script editor, that mainly pertain to lines actors are having problems with, cleaning up a few leftover continuity issues (but these will be minor), and sometimes dealing with bigger issues like a script spreading in rehearsal (so that you need to make clever trims) or (which is worse) shrinking so that it now needs to have material added to it.

There is rarely more than one day's rehearsal in any long-running drama's production schedule. Soaps, in particular, tend to 'rehearse, record'. Which means actors do not have rehearsal days set aside in the schedule, but must have their lines learned before shooting commences (or be 'off the script').

The rehearsal script is the draft used at the all-important read-through, the one day set aside in the busy production schedule of a series or serial drama for the cast, heads of department, director, producer, executive producer, script editor, and you, the writer, to gather together to read the block of episodes through. Any problems – editorial, creative, financial or production-related – are aired here.

It is at this read-through that you will find out whether your dialogue truly flows, and you are at liberty to make suggested line changes via your script editor, who will get sign off from the producer and executive producer before the new pages (which will be colour-coded) are inserted into the script, ready for its final metamorphosis.

SHOOTING SCRIPT

The PA (production assistant) is now, at this stage in your script's life, often liaising with your script editor about timings. This is the first thing a PA does with a new script from a new block of episodes that are due to be shot.

To make your script truly camera ready, it must:

- have the requisite number of interior (INT) and exterior (EXT) scenes
- be to time

The interior scenes in a typical soap script will be allocated to the interior sets, which fall into two categories: those that are PERMANENT and those that are FLOATING.

Within the studio, there will be the larger, more complicated sets (like the interior of the Queen Vic, for instance) and the smaller, more portable ones (like the sitting room of one of the houses). The floating sets are removed or re-established as the episodes dictate.

The exterior scenes on a soap are defined as those that are on the LOT, or permanently fixed for outside shooting (Albert Square in the case of *EastEnders*, or The Street in the case of *Coronation Street*), and those exterior scenes which are categorised as LOCATION.

Location scenes on a fast-turnaround show like *EastEnders* form a very small percentage (less than 25 per cent) of the scene count in a typical script. Location is expensive and miles travelled to the shoot are strictly limited by budget, as are the shooting days.

The scenes in a typical shooting script will be divided, then, between the following sets:

INT: Floating or Permanent
EXT: Location or Lot

A typical *EastEnders* episode for the BBC comes in at around 28 minutes. Some directors like to work with a little more or a little less material, but this is a good ballpark figure, which is then cut to accommodate the credit sequence and titles lasting 58 seconds. As a script editor on *EastEnders*, one of the things I made sure each script had was a great exit line of dialogue, or an image, or a close-up, just as those famous drum beats were heard coming in over the credit sequence.

A typical *Emmerdale* episode for ITV comes in at around 23 minutes, including cuts made for the credits and three advertising breaks. The first advertising break comes about 7 minutes into the episode, the second one at 15 minutes in, and the last one at 23 minutes. This is the cliffhanger break. Writers use the advertising structure to shape their episodes and storylines accordingly.

Writing on a returning series or soap is both hard work and hugely rewarding.

You are protected to a large extent from making time-costly mistakes (not fulfilling the brief arising from each draft's note session, for example) by the attention and care given to you and your script by your assigned script editor.

The ratings on our most popular continuing dramas (*EastEnders*, *Coronation Street* and *Emmerdale*) regularly exceed seven million and, for *Corrie*, that figure has recently crept above nine million. If you want to get really good, really quickly, at creating and delivering stories and characters that a large chunk of the population can relate to and get your name out there, on screen, to be seen by millions of people per week, then writing on a soap, or one of the series juggernauts, is the way forward for you.

STAY **POSITIVE**

Television eats writers. And stories. There's so much drama to be made, and usually not enough time or quite enough money to make it.

However, producers all need good writers and they are keen to establish relationships with writers who are not only talented, but reliable, good to work with and collaborative.

Use the Radio Times: *http://www.radiotimes.com/tv*
Sounds a bit odd to say it, but here you will find listed producers, executive producers and script editors of the long-running shows and serial formats.

Use the online publication Contacts:
http://www.contactshandbook.com
This lists production companies from across the entertainment industry, together with their contact details. You will find companies like Kay Mellor's Rollem, Red Productions, Tiger Aspect and Kudos, in addition to the smaller concerns and bigger independents. Firstly, find out if these companies will read unsolicited work – not all do.

Broadcast magazine: *http://www.broadcastnow.co.uk*
This is a useful source of information about who is making what and when. The subscription isn't cheap, but I think it's worth the outlay.

Network on social networking sites
Maximise your contacts – don't be a weirdo but do encourage those you admire in the industry to connect with you.

Scriptwriting competitions

Definitely, in my view, a very good way of getting your work read and assessed, getting practised and good at meeting deadlines, and honing your writing skill. You will find that script editors and producers will have their eyes on the good ones out there. So if you are placed, or even long-listed, all to the good for getting your name into the television corporate consciousness! Here are some that I rate:

- **Red Planet Prize:**
  http://www.redplanetpictures.co.uk/opportunities.php
- **Scriptwriting Goldmine:** *http://awards.screenwritinggoldmine.com/*
- **BBC Writersroom:** *http://www.bbc.co.uk/writersroom/opportunities/*
- **Blue Cat Screenplay:** *http://www.bluecatscreenplay.com/*
- **Euroscript:** *http://www.euroscript.co.uk*

Enjoy television

These are some of my favourite shows, all of them commercial, all appealing to a wide audience base, and some still retaining the quirky element in spite of having to attract healthy ratings:

- *Broadchurch*
- *The Syndicate*
- *Last Tango in Halifax*
- *Call the Midwife*
- *Roger and Val Have Just Got In*
- *Holby City*
- *Coronation Street*
- *The Accused*
- *Silent Witness*
- *Being Human*
- *Skins*

Do not get disheartened if you are finding you are up against some closed doors. At the risk of repeating myself, television eats writers. So, if you don't mind being gobbled up by a huge story-generating machine, you need to make sure that your script is strong and that you are confident, and just keep knocking on those doors. There will be a script editor or a producer behind one of them with whom your work will resonate.

Remember: be prepared to be collaborative, work to deadline, and hone your storylining and treatment-writing skills – so you can create commercially viable, engaging formats.

TELEVISION WRITERS TALK
ABOUT TELEVISION WRITING

I can talk about the world of television writing till I'm blue in the face and do it with conviction. However, my point of view is that of a script editor, a producer, a developer of drama for television. Here, I give the floor (and a chapter) to the writers who are doing the job of getting words on our screens day in, day out.

I chat with Damon, Sally, Lisa, Pete and Robert: the writers of *Coronation Street*, *Casualty*, *Holby City*, *EastEnders* and *Emmerdale* (amongst other shows) talking about the highs and the lows of this testing, but rewarding, business.

DAMON ROCHEFORT – *CORONATION STREET*

'Never give up.'

Damon talks about the circuitous route he followed onto his favourite television show:

I'd been in the music business for many years and had a series of hits as Nomad ('I Wanna Give You Devotion' being the biggest), as well as writing and producing for Kim Wilde, Bad Boys Inc, La Toya Jackson and many others. But I always wanted to write for TV. I was slightly obsessed with *Roseanne*, *Cheers*, *Golden Girls* and *The Mary Tyler Moore Show*, and one of my best friends, Helen Smith (now an established author), suggested I go on an Arvon residential writing course. The tutors for that particular sit-com course were comedy gods Laurence Marks and Maurice Gran (*Birds of a Feather*, *New Statesman*, *Goodnight Sweetheart*) and, after a fantastic week, they suggested that I write a spec script for one of their shows to see – in their words – if I could walk the walk as well as talk the talk.

When I got home, I wrote a *Birds of a Feather* script, with no training or experience whatsoever, and sent it to them within a few days. They liked it very much and said they'd keep me in mind in future. But, in an extremely fortunate bit of serendipity, I got a call from their office a few days later to say that a writer on the current series of *Birds*, which they were filming, had dropped out and could they use my script as ep two of the new series? I said yes, of course, thinking, 'Gosh, that was easy,' and the next week I was down at a rehearsal room, at a table read of my script with the *Birds* cast and crew.

This stuff does not happen as a rule, as an amused Mo and Lo have pointed out to me many times over the years, but it was a combination of naive confidence on my part on the one hand, and a series of fortunate events on the other.

They encouraged me to write my own sit-com after that, but then my naivety and confidence were as much a drawback as a strength, as I had no idea of the difficulty of a guy with very little experience (two eps of *Birds* by now) getting his own show away.

The only other show I really wanted to write was *Corrie*, but again my lack of experience was against me. I phoned Granada and asked for the opportunity to write a spec script, which I did. And they turned me down. Nicely, I might add. But I asked to write another, and they said they usually asked new writers to wait at least 12 months before doing another trial, but I pleaded and begged, and they relented and let me do another straightaway. Which they also turned down; but they told me it was much better than the first and gave me excellent notes. I blush remembering it, but I pleaded and begged to do a third trial, and they must have taken pity on me because they let me do one. Which they turned down again, though, by this time, they had made it clear that they liked my writing very much, particularly – and

I can't stress the importance of this enough for writers starting out – as I clearly understood the tone of the show, and my love of the characters and the show really shone through. This is vital! Don't try and get on a show unless you know it inside out. It's insulting to the show and those that work on it if you're clueless about the show you're trying to write for.

I'd sort of given up hope by now, so I sent my last *Corrie* trial script to *Family Affairs*, and they immediately asked me to write a double episode, which I was thrilled about. I sent a 'thank you' note to *Corrie*, telling them this, as it was their notes and encouragement that had helped me to develop my writing so much, and got a response back from the producer at the time asking me to go and see him for a chat.

I finished my *Family Affairs* double, went to see the producer at *Corrie* and, after a lively meeting, he asked me to attend the next Story Conference. Nine years and about 150 eps later, and here I am, still writing for the show I love the best on British TV.

The lesson? Never give up, listen to notes, believe in yourself and develop your talent. But above all? Never give up.

Robert and Sally both got their original break into television writing from the BBC Academy, as it was under John Yorke. I include their interviews here because they are both such marvellous examples of how training schemes really work:

ROBERT GOLDSBROUGH – Writer and BBC Writer Trainee

'It's amazing, actually, how many people are out there, willing to help you out.'

Robert talks here about how important it is to value those that give you a leg up:

What are you working on at the moment?

Right now I'm just starting to work on my episode of *Casualty* and will go on to do a *Holby City* followed by a stint in the *EastEnders* story office before writing an episode of that, too. But you don't get any special treatment. If you don't cut it on your episodes, you can be replaced at any time, just like every other writer. We get a shot, but there are no guarantees beyond that.

What is the best thing about writing for an established series?

It's great to get to write for some truly iconic characters that you've grown up watching your entire life. Whether it's Dot Cotton or Charlie Fairhead, suddenly you get to put words into their mouths. It's almost like playing with the BBC's toys! There's a huge weight of history behind them and incredible production teams who know exactly what works and what doesn't from years of experience. These are really popular shows, too, with massive audiences. Some people dream of playing at Wembley, but an episode of *EastEnders* allows you to play for an audience up to a hundred times that size. That's a big responsibility, but, to quote Matthew Graham, it's also a privilege. No matter what else you might be working on, at least everyone's heard of *EastEnders*!

Are there any downsides?

When you're dealing with long-running shows that produce 40, 50, or over 200 episodes every year, it can be difficult to find new territory to explore. No matter how good or how original you think an idea you have is, chances are it's been done three times before and is coming up again in a few weeks! So you have to work really hard to find fresh angles and unexpected twists. Some people on the outside looking in might think it's easy, but it's anything but. There are lots of logistics to consider, like cast and set availability, scheduling and so forth. It's also a huge machine that can swallow you up if you don't fight to hold on to your voice. But these are the challenges every writer has to meet head on if they're to succeed – I'm certainly still learning how to get it right.

What television drama most influenced your decision to write for television?

I should probably name something very worthy and earnest but, if anything, it's probably *The X-Files*. It was really intelligently written and had such an elasticity of format – it could be dark horror one week and extravagant comedy the next. It told standalone stories as well as having a long-form mythology, and I really think its influence on television has been underestimated. There are all sorts of other shows that have influenced me, too – Jimmy McGovern's *The Street* and, more recently, *Accused* are perfect examples of gripping human drama without the need for any external story machine. Then there are US series like *Breaking Bad*, which is just incredible.

Who do you admire in the television writing industry?

I sometimes have to remind myself how lucky I've been to meet, however briefly, so many writers that I really admire – Jimmy McGovern, Peter Bowker, Sarah Phelps, Frank Spotnitz, Ryan Murphy, Jack Thorne, to name just a few. They've all offered words of wisdom and their work is a constant influence and inspiration. Sometimes you hear that the industry is a closed shop, but it's amazing, actually, how many people are out there, willing to help you out.

SALLY ABBOTT – *CASUALTY*

'The ambition and aim for it to be brilliant has to be there. It's not fair on the audience or the team behind it otherwise. If you don't care passionately, then why should they?'

Sally has a baptism of fire on Casualty:

I'd got on to the shadow scheme for *EastEnders* already. What I did not expect, therefore, when I started to write Casualty, was that I would totally fall in love with the show.

I had a bit of a baptism of fire. A brilliant stunt had been suggested to me – a rollercoaster accident. My script editor had heard from the art director that it would be relatively easy to do, so I created a story around that. All was going well after a slightly eggy start, mainly due to me doing my own head in with the crippling doubt that I couldn't do it, as well as a spectacular lack of preparation on my part. We were a week away from shooting when the amusement park, where we were filming the rollercoaster accident, pulled out. Unsurprisingly, they didn't want to be associated with a huge accident and six deaths – even if the storyline was very clearly about sabotage.

The team brainstormed possible stunts they knew they could afford, could arrange in less than a week, and which wouldn't change the medicine moving forward too much. I was given a choice of three disasters including, 'We think we can recreate the ending of *The Italian Job* – you know, the coach hanging over a cliff?' I asked if we could push the coach over the cliff. A bit of confabbing later and they said yes. It meant I had about three days to rewrite it to reflect the new stunt.

The stunt looked brilliant!

I do love *Casualty* to bits. There's so much I can say!

I also go into filming when I can and often talk directly to the actors about it on the floor and then rewrite – even whilst filming.

So, for example, on my second ep, 'Eliminate the Negative' (which got me all my other eps of *Casualty*), I saw that my guest lead, Rudi Valentino (played by the scarily talented Sean Cernow), was just absolutely incredible. Just amazing. I'd written the part for him anyway, and had crossed my fingers he'd get it. It was an unusual ep as he was the main character in the whole episode. This was at a point when the main stories weren't really patient ones, more staff-related ones. Mark Catley, the show's then series script editor, gave me full permission to run with Rudi being big. I remember asking at commissioning if we could have a guest character this big and Mark said, 'You can when he's like this.' Rudi was a manic force of nature, a total knobhead who you started the ep being incredibly annoyed with, and by the end you've completely fallen in love with him. It was obvious watching filming that a bit of his journey was missing – the very last bit. So I wrote a new ending scene for him where he died – very quietly, very calmly – in Resus with just Zoe with him. It was heartbreaking.

The fact I can go on set, meet the actors, discuss with them, rewrite scenes, and that Wendy Wright (our scheduler) then manages to schedule them is just amazing. And this is bearing in mind that this is continuing drama – where time, space, actors, the schedule and money are totally, totally overstretched.

My main thing always about writing *Casualty* (and writing in general) is that you have to greet it with an enormous passion and a desire to make it the best it can possibly be. I'm not saying that what I do is brilliant, or the best or anything – I'm always gutted I didn't find better story solutions, or when I have lines that sound hollow or things that don't work. But the ambition and aim for it to be brilliant has to be there. It's not fair on the audience or the team behind it otherwise. If you don't care passionately, then why should they?

LISA HOLDSWORTH – *EMMERDALE/MIDSOMER MURDERS*

'It was a tough learning curve, but I got there in the end.'

Lisa's hard work and persistence pays off:

Whilst I was doing my film studies degree in London, I realised that I didn't want to be an actor any more. They get told what to do too much, and I wanted to do the telling. So, when I should have been writing my dissertation, I started writing a script called *Jackie's Wedding*. And I actually finished it! I carried on working on it when I got back to Leeds and started working in factual TV. So, when I realised I was working with Kay Mellor's son-in-law, I had a script that I could shove into his hands and ask him to put on his mother-in-law's reading pile. Which is exactly what he did. Kay then told me that she really thought I could write, but I did need more practice.

She gave me a writing trial on *Playing the Field*, but I didn't get the job because of lack of experience. A few months later, I became Kay's PA and, when she decided to make a second series of *Fat Friends*, I pitched an idea for an episode. And that became my first commission. It was a tough learning curve, but I got to the end and actually got the episode broadcast! From there I took a job at *Emmerdale* and really learned how to write for telly. And the rest, as they say, is history.

PETE LAWSON – *EASTENDERS*

'I get to sit in my room and write "He falls through the burning floor" – and someone makes it happen. It's magic!'

Pete takes us through some of the rigours of writing on a juggernaut:

What is the best thing about writing for *EastEnders*?

I love that we can get the country talking – and sometimes change or reframe the public debate about issues. I always think that's one of the things soap does best – it entertains, it provides escapism, it gives you great stories, but it gets people on their sofas and in their schools and in their workplaces talking. That's a real privilege to be part of. I remember working as a volunteer on a gay helpline in the 1990s when Tiffany's boyfriend, Tony, was struggling with his sexuality – I was on the phones the night he came out, and all evening we had people ringing, saying it'd just given them the courage to come out to their families/girlfriends/best mates. When we get it right – like with Mark's HIV, Whitney's various abuse stories, Dot and Ethel and euthanasia, or with Syed struggling to be gay and a Muslim – it changes how people see themselves, and the world around them. And if that leads to the world being a better, more open and tolerant place – what a privilege to be part of.

I love having a platform to entertain seven, eight, nine million people and more – three of my eps have got over 11 million viewers. I can't even picture what that many people looks like. I come from theatre – from fringe theatre initially – where you might get 50 people in a room listening to your words, watching them acted out. So to have the privilege of sharing something I've created with that many viewers – it's amazing. To have a chance to make that many people laugh, that many people cry; to take that many people on a bit of a journey after a long day – you don't get that chance that often.

I love our actors. I think we've got one of the strongest ensemble casts of any show on TV – so to get to write for them, week on week, is hugely exciting. Don't ask me who my favourites are – don't want jealous actors on my case! We've got legends on there like June Brown. I get to put words in Dot Cotton's mouth. Life doesn't get much better than that.

I love being part of a team – being a writer can be a lonely job at times, so to have so many really lovely, talented people to interact with on a regular basis is brilliant. It's a family, a home, and that's great.

And, finally, it's fun! At heart, we tell stories about people and families and relationships, and those big, emotional pieces are the ones I'm proudest of. But I've also blown up buildings, thrown people off piers, collapsed restaurants on top of lovers. I get to sit in my room and write 'He falls through the burning floor' – and someone makes it happen. It's magic!

Do you find the structure you obviously have to adhere to on the programme a restriction, or do you find you use it to your own advantage?

I guess a bit of both. Of course, the show has a long-established structure – we tell multiple stories in an intertwined way; we build towards a cliff, creating mini cliffs along the way. Then individual episodes have their own restrictions – actors' availability, which sets are in the studios that week, and so on.

So you embrace all that. There's no point complaining you can't play rugby if you're on a football pitch. If you want to play rugby, then go off and play it. Write that novel, or that film, or develop your own series in your own way. But if you've been invited to play on the football pitch, then that's the game, those are the rules – so embrace them, seize the opportunity, and play the best game of football that's ever been played. As a writer, over the course of your career, you get to write many things in many different ways – that's one of the joys of being a writer.

What you've got with *EastEnders* is a structure that works; a set of characters who work, who have depth and complexity, and lives and history, and distinct voices and traits. All the things that, if you're creating your own material, you spend months trying to get right (and often failing to). Then, here you are, with a structure that works, with characters who work. How can that be a restriction? You take the stories you've got, and tell them in that particular way. And enjoy making that dialogue as characterful as possible.

And sometimes the restrictions push your creativity, which is always a good thing. If you can't do something in the most obvious way, in the way you first thought of – because those characters can't cross in that particular location, for instance, or that character's not available – then you have to look for more interesting ways to tell that story. Which almost always makes the script better.

There's a lot at stake these days, with the need to keep your show top of the ratings. Do you find the writers have to work very closely with the producers to come up with great storylines to keep the audience figures high?

The producers are ultimately the ones in charge; they have to set the direction and the tone, lead the team in deciding what stories to tell, what characters to introduce, which characters to let go. They're the ones who have to answer to the critics and the BBC bosses – they deservedly get the plaudits when we get it right, as they're the ones who ultimately carry the can when we get it wrong.

But, having said that, the producers work incredibly closely with the writers. The key writers and producers meet up regularly to look at the stories we're telling, to pitch new ideas, to argue about what's working and what isn't. To keep on top of the game as a show, you've got to have as many different voices and viewpoints and ideas as you can in the room – without it all getting so big that it becomes unmanageable, or loses focus, or dilutes a vision. Writers tend to throw ideas around, look at the bigger arcs; then we have story producers and a story team who work closely with our lead writer/ story consultant to pull that together into a week-by-week, day-by-day structure that works.

Can you talk a little about the Story Conference?

I always find the Story Conference table tough, but fun. It's always scary, coming up with an idea, then putting it in front of other people. You worry that what you've come up with is rubbish or clichéd or simply dull. At its worst, it becomes gladiatorial – people pitching, only for others to rip those ideas apart. But most of the time at *EastEnders* – and certainly at present – it's much more collaborative, much more creative. People pitch, the group explores – you might keep some elements, lose others, combine with other ideas, take a story and decide it would work better with a different character. I think that culture of shooting things down because you don't like the person pitching, or people playing power games, jostling for position, has really changed. We're all there for the same reason – to make the show as good as it can be.

At the end of the day, we need to challenge each other's ideas, interrogate a concept, make sure stories are going to work; but, like most stuff in life, better things come from people working together than against each other. Two heads can achieve so much more than one – it's not just that you've got two ideas; you've also got that bit of magic that happens when those two heads work together, and you create something that no one would ever have thought of on their own. And for two heads, of course, read four, eight, sixteen... You need that creative soup. Even if someone just brings a little bit of salt, that's the bit that makes the whole difference. You never know where the solution to that story problem's going to come from, but you can guarantee it's in the room somewhere, waiting to be found.

Do you find the deadlines helpful, or a hindrance to the writing process?

For me, they're completely helpful. I work best to a deadline. You have to get something down – even if you leave it till the last minute, you have to get it written. Then that gives you the adrenalin needed to dig down inside and find something hopefully brilliant. If I don't work to deadline, I hardly ever get things done. I have projects of my own that just sit there for years. Something in your head sparks differently when you're up against it. I think it makes you dig down deeper. To trust your instinct. And that's where the magic lies.

Ask me again on a Sunday afternoon when I've been writing all weekend and everyone else is down at the beach. Then maybe I'll give you a different answer about deadlines.

How did you start your writing journey on *EastEnders*?

I started in June 2008. I've written for TV since 1995, when I was part of a Carlton-run course for young writers (which was where I first met the lovely Yvonne Grace!). They'd spotted me in theatre, and invited me to develop a screenplay. From there, they commissioned a half-hour comedy called *Sweet*, about a young gay couple with fidelity issues. It was made by Verity Lambert, who inspired and terrified me in equal measures. She was a god of TV drama, and I was a bit in awe. But it was a fantastic opportunity, and the end result was great. Just seeing my words on screen for the first time. Amazing.

The year after, Carlton launched a London-based soap called *London Bridge*, and I became a core writer on that for a couple of years. I then did a brief stint on *Casualty*, worked on the short-lived but rather fantastic soap *Night and Day*, and started developing my own work. In 2002 I was very lucky to get my own BBC series off the ground, called *Being April*. It starred Pauline Quirke as a single mum with three kids by three dads – one of whom was Asian, one of whom was gay. Nitin Ganatra, who currently plays Masood in *EastEnders*, actually played one of the dads in *Being April*.

I wrote an afternoon play for the BBC called *Drive*, and after that I spent a couple of years developing new ideas for the BBC, and then a couple of years with Mal Young at 19TV (who make *American Idol*), developing ideas for the UK and the USA. It was all a lot of fun, but development can be exhausting – you put a lot out there, and get very little back. I had a string of scripts which, for many reasons, ended up not getting made – some would have been wonderful; one or two pretty much stank. As a writer, I needed to do something different.

I was desperate to write something again that got made, to work with a team, and to have a chance just to write without having to come up with my own stories and concepts for a while. *EastEnders* was the only programme I wanted to write for – I've watched it since it launched. I love the characters, I love the stories we tell. It's all about relationships and family, which is what I write best – and when we get it right, it has that mix of humour and drama that I love.

So I asked my agent to set up a meeting for me. At that time they ran a shadow scheme for writers who were new to the show. You got given the same storylines as an existing writer, and got to write your own version of a script. If they felt you got the show, and got the character voices, then they offered you a commission. That's what happened to me, and so I joined the writing team. The first ep I had revolved around the Masoods – who were my favourite characters at the time – and their battle to keep the post office. They continued to offer me more episodes, then after a while invited me to join the core team. Forty-nine episodes later (at the time of writing), and I'm still here!

Do you find working so closely on a juggernaut like *EastEnders* a daunting job for a writer, or an opportunity to get your voice out there?

Both. It's daunting because you're responsible for one of the country's biggest shows. It's been running well over 25 years, it regularly gets the biggest audiences of the week – you know more people are watching your work than anything else that day. You know you're writing for fans who love the show, who are passionate, who feel that they own it. And who, through the licence fee, pay for it. So to carry that baton and not drop it, that's daunting. But get it right, and it's the best gig in the world.

And anything that lets you write and gets your work made and your words on screen and seen by an audience – of course, that's all part of getting your voice out there. There are other things I've written, more signature things, which might have a purer version of my voice. But that's the name of the game – you're writing on a huge team show, not penning your own little personal poem. There's not a single episode I've written that I've not been enormously proud of.

That hasn't felt like my voice. That hasn't given me such a kick to see my name on the credits.

Can you talk a little about the relationship you have with your script editor? Your producer? Other writers on the team?

Some of the best script editors I've ever worked with have been on *EastEnders*. It's an invaluable relationship, a really crucial one. Whatever you're writing, you need someone who looks at your work and helps you see what is and isn't working. It's no good arguing what a scene's about – if it's not actually in the scene, if it's not what's coming across to a reader, then it's not there, and you need to rework it. If a line doesn't make sense, it doesn't make sense! Argue all you like, but, if someone doesn't get it, then it's your job to make sure they do. If it's not coming across to a script editor, it won't come across on screen.

A script editor's job is to help you make the stories work, both in your particular episode and across that week as a whole. It's also their job to know what's played the week before and what's playing the week after – as a writer, you get an outline, but things change along the way. And, even if stories haven't changed, there might be scenes or conversations or even just lines that are the same as things you've written.

A good script editor will help you cut something down to size, make sure the characters' voices are strong and clear, that your jokes work, that your emotional stuff isn't overwritten. It can be a fractious relationship – no one likes to hear criticism – and they're also gathering all sorts of views from research, producers, directors, and trying to channel these to you as some kind of cohesive whole. And they're usually doing that across about eight different episodes at once – it's an impossible job, in some ways a thankless job, but absolutely vital to the creation of a brilliant show and to the shaping of a great script.

Don't think of it as a battle – two people trying to drag a script in two different directions – but as a genuine collaboration. You've both got the same goal – to create the best episode you possibly can. So you have to learn to listen to each other, to explore together what isn't working, and figure out how to make it better. You have to respect each other's roles and skills and knowledge. Whatever you write, however good it is, it can always be better. Always. And that's their job. They're on your side.

As a writer, you don't get that much direct contact with a producer. They'll give their notes and thoughts to your script editor. Obviously, they're looking at the overall shape and tone of the show – they've got a level of overview and oversight that you'll never have, and they know the show inside out. So, again, it's important to listen to them. It doesn't mean your viewpoint as a writer doesn't count, but I can't say it often enough – it's a team show. And a team of hugely talented people – so why wouldn't you want to listen to that?

And other writers – usually, you'll meet them just once a month when you get commissioned to write a new episode and get together with the team to talk through the stories you've got. Sometimes you email or call each other as you're writing, just to check how something's being played – sometimes you'll do that through a script editor. And many of the writers I've been lucky enough to work with at *EastEnders* I'd now call my friends. It's a great team, and a real pleasure to be part of.

THE BBC SHADOW SCHEME,
WITH GLEN LAKER

The BBC Shadow Scheme offers new writers who have talent, but lack production experience, the chance to find out what it is like working on a commissioned show. Here, I talk to one of its recent recruits.

Could you tell me what started you writing, where your passion comes from, and how long you've been pursuing a career in television writing?

I'm not sure what started me writing. I've always had a good imagination. I was always a daydreamer, especially at school. I used to make up stories as a kid and I can remember writing short stories even at primary-school age that I'd read to my parents. I also wrote sketches for school assemblies, stuff like that. When I was 16 or 17, a friend gave me a copy of the screenplay for Tim Burton's *Batman*. It was an early draft by Sam Hamm. I'd never read a screenplay before. This was before the Internet and databases of PDFs made it easy to get your hands on screenplays. This Sam Hamm script was a barely legible bootleg, a photocopy of a photocopy of a photocopy. But the way it was written really struck a chord with me. The immediacy of the language. The way everything was so visual and in the present tense. It was all meat and no fat and I loved that and still do. It was art. Like a verbal comic book. I think screenplay writing is an underrated art form. I read a lot of scripts and so many of them are better written than the books on the bestseller lists.

So after I read that Sam Hamm *Batman* script, I started to write my own screenplays. I wrote lots of them. All of them awful.

So cut forward five years; I left film school and wanted to be a writer-director. I made a couple of short films but then graduated towards writing. I got a few writing jobs alongside the day jobs. I'd write in my breaks, at evenings and weekends. The usual story. I was mainly writing feature films and I was lucky to get a few sales. I adapted a James Herbert bestseller (*Sepulchre*) and also wrote a sci-fi thriller (*Bluebird*) which sold in LA. It was all very exciting, but felt like a hobby.

About four years ago, I started to look seriously at writing for television. To be honest, I was desperate to get something produced! I'd watched four feature-length projects roll over and die and I didn't want to go through that process again. So I set myself a five-year target to write for a primetime show. I wrote a sitcom pilot and sent it out to a few producers. It got some good feedback and someone at the BBC suggested I apply to the BBC Writers Academy.

So I did. Twice. And twice I didn't make the shortlist. I was and am a huge fan of *Holby City*, so I really wanted to write for that show in particular. I'd read a couple of the show's scripts and they were written in a familiar filmic language, which really appealed. So, in 2012, I started looking into the various shadow writing schemes that the BBC runs and applied for the *Holby City* scheme.

What dramas/writers inspire you to write for television?

I remember watching Jimmy McGovern's *Cracker* and then *The Lakes* and just being blown away by his writing. Similarly, Alan Bleasdale's *GBH*, which was one of the first shows I'd rush home to catch. For me it's usually the big tent-pole dramas that stick in my mind. Lynda La Plante's *Prime Suspect* and Anthony Minghella's sublime work on *Inspector Morse* are two other fine examples. Also I'm a huge fan of the BBC's remake of *Wallander*.

Lately, I can't get enough of US shows like *Generation Kill*, *Breaking Bad*, *Battlestar Galactica* and *The Wire*. I think Aaron Sorkin's *The West Wing* and *The Newsroom* are enviably good, too.

I thought the first series of both *The Bridge* (the original Swedish/ Danish series) and *The Killing* (both Swedish and US versions) were wonderfully structured.

How did you get on to the Shadow Scheme? Was there a filter system you had to go through or were you approached via the BBC Writersroom having submitted a script? Is there an application process?

I applied! The BBC advertised the scheme on the BBC Jobs website. They requested a CV and a sample of writing. I'd just finished a 60-minute drama pilot for the Red Planet Prize, so I used that.

They did want applications through an agent, which I guess is a filtering system of sorts. As I remember it, they read the first ten pages of the sample scripts and made a longlist of writers. The BBC then read the full scripts and made a shortlist of 12–15 writers, who were then invited to an interview with Simon Harper, who was, at the time, script producer (he's now the show's senior producer) at *Holby City*'s production offices in Elstree. That was basically a standard job interview, with questions thrown in to make sure I knew the show's plots and characters.

Do you have an agent?

The BBC Shadow Scheme only accepts applications from represented writers, which can seem unfair. When I first read about the post on the BBC Jobs site, I didn't have an agent. So the first thing I did was set about finding one. I was lucky to find one in the nick of time.

Writing a script for a drama goliath like *Holby* is no mean feat. You must be really excited to have had the opportunity. Can you take me through the rough process that you went through to write your episode?

Each episode of *Holby City* is broken into A, B and C story strands. For the scheme, you write just the A story, which is more or less half of a script, so 30 minutes' worth. The first stage is a lot of reading. You are sent about six months' worth of story documents to catch up on, with character biographies, floor plans of the sets and some medical notes. For me, this was the most difficult part of the process because it was just days upon days of reading and note-taking.

Then you're given your episode storyline. This is broken down into five acts and gives you your main beats for your regular characters. You do a verbal pitch to your script editor/producer about your guest characters and how you see them weaving into your episode.

The next stage is to write your 'beatsheet', which is a scene-by-scene account of your episode, written as a prose document. This is where the fun starts and you start to feel your episode is taking shape.

You get notes back and revise your beatsheet, then you go to script. On the Shadow Scheme we did three drafts, but on the actual show it's usually five. You get notes after each draft and discuss your changes/revisions with your script editor/producer, then you're given a week or two to do the rewrite.

Were there any nasty surprises waiting in store for you, or did you pretty much stay on track throughout the process of writing, having your script edited, and then delivering to deadline?

For the Shadow Scheme, you're pretty protected from the nasty surprises, because your script isn't going to go into production. But the notes really push you to go as far as you can with your characters and storylines.

But after the Shadow Scheme, when I got to write on the show for real, I had a few surprises. Writing on continuing drama is like jumping on to a moving conveyor belt. The deadlines are a shock at first, but then you just adapt to them. I was used to being given months on a draft; on *Holby*, it's a couple of weeks, sometimes less.

I was used to the script-editing process, having developed a handful of feature projects and also having worked as a script editor on some other television dramas. But one thing I will say is the people who work on *Holby* are a lovely bunch and they want you to write the best episode ever, which can seem daunting, but once you hand in that final draft, you feel you've at least written the best episode you could have.

Oh, then there's actor availability, which was a new thing for me. I had to do an urgent rewrite of a whole strand because the actor who played one of my main characters was no longer available for the shoot. That's when writing becomes something more like puzzle-solving.

If you have written single-format screenplays before, could you tell me, from the writer's perspective, what the biggest differences are in writing a long-run format like *Holby City*, as opposed to the single-episode story?

Structurally, it took me a while to get my head around how hard 60 minutes of continuing drama is to write.

Coming from a feature-film background, writing on *Holby* was a steep learning curve. There were times when I would stare at the story documents and wonder what I was doing. When you're used to writing spec scripts from your own ideas, it can actually be a blessing to be given the rough storyline. But often your storyline is top level, so breaking it down into individual scenes and beats can seem insurmountable.

Then you have the restrictions: obviously you have 60 minutes to fit it all into, but within that you have to balance your A, B and C storylines across the episode. Also, you might be told that certain characters can't cross, because of actor availability.

What is the next step for you and your writing?

I've got some other projects that have gone into development with television companies since I finished the *Holby* scheme. Also, my feature, *Bluebird*, is going from strength to strength in LA, so I'm now lucky enough to be writing full-time. That's certainly something I didn't think would happen two years ago.

Do you think the Shadow Scheme has helped you along your way?

Definitely. Just getting onto the scheme gave me a huge boost of confidence. I'd pretty much given up on ever writing full-time. So I couldn't believe it when I got onto the scheme, especially because

I'd applied to similar schemes before and failed. And, of course, the sheer number of writers who apply is staggering.

It opens doors. Because these shows are so tough to work on, I think if you can get through the Shadow Scheme, it puts you in good stead to work on other shows. Plus, you learn so much from doing it. I realised how little I knew about my writing and it really helped me when the producers and script editors on *Holby* pushed me to my limits, because I came out the other end thinking, 'Wow, did I really write that?' For a writer, that's a great feeling.

In terms of getting hands-on experience of working as a writer on a commissioned show, how do you rate the BBC Shadow Scheme?

Ten out of ten! I think if you're looking to break into television, the opportunities are few and far between. There are a lot of prizes which promise you a break, but they rarely deliver. So these Shadow Schemes, or similar schemes where you write a dummy episode, are tremendous. They're a great platform on which you can prove to the commissioners that you're worth a shot on their shows.

YOUR STORY, ON TELEVISION –
TALKING WITH DEBBIE MOON

Debbie Moon created and wrote the CBBC hit *Wolfblood*. *Wolfblood* won the RTS Award for Best Children's Programme, and was nominated for four BAFTAs, winning one (Best Performer). It's been sold to Disney and is currently showing in the US and around 40 other countries worldwide.

Here I talk to Debbie about the development process and what makes writing for children's channels so rewarding.

What's the best thing about writing children's drama?

Probably the best thing is the openness to big ideas. In primetime television, science fiction and fantasy go in and out of fashion; in children's television, there's always a place for it, and a real understanding of how fantasy elements can illuminate the real world and real-life decisions.

The great thing about science fiction and fantasy is that their very 'unreality' allows you to explore real issues in a very direct way. *Wolfblood* may be about kids who can turn into wolves, but it's actually about fitting in, being different, deciding how to live, building a 'family' for yourself when you don't have one. Because of that fantasy metaphor, we can tackle big issues quite directly, while keeping it fun and dramatic – and children's television is very much the place to do that.

What's the most difficult thing?

Obviously there are things you can't do in a children's programme; we must be the only werewolf drama ever where no one gets so much as bitten! That can be difficult. When serious violence is off the table, you have to find inventive ways to threaten the characters and ramp up the drama.

And we work pretty hard to achieve the look of the show, and the special effects, on a limited budget. We film in the north of England very early in the year, do a lot of exteriors, and do more night shoots than any other children's drama, all of which plays havoc with the schedule and the budget.

So a lot of very precise rewriting can be required to tell the story in a way we can afford to shoot, and that can be frustrating. Good ideas have to be abandoned or watered down; you have to compromise on the visuals or the locations. But, in the end, television is about practical storytelling, and there's nothing like restrictions to force you to be inventive!

You are in the enviable position of having had your work developed and taken to a full series by CBBC – can you tell me something about this process?

Wolfblood was commissioned after I submitted it via a BBC Writersroom scheme, so at the time I only had a rough draft of a first episode. No character profiles, no idea where the story was going next. So a lot of the development process was about exploring the characters and defining the world of the story.

Working with an existing concept, you have to be clear on what your take on it is, and what it was that attracted you to it in the first place. I knew from the beginning that I wanted to reinvent certain elements of traditional werewolf stories. Being a Wolfblood wouldn't be an affliction or a curse, but a natural part of you, even an enjoyable 'gift' – albeit one that had to be hidden from most humans. So we spent quite a lot of time working out what the Wolfblood world was like: how they lived, exactly what abilities they had in human form, how the transformations worked.

And sometimes you have to work your way through a more complicated version of your idea to get to the simple version. At one stage we developed an entire hierarchy of the Wolfblood world, with various authority figures and a kind of police force that protected the secret – but we realised that was shifting the emphasis from the child characters to the adults, so we simplified the story again and concentrated on events within this one village, this one family.

Wolfblood was in development for nearly two years – partly because the development process was running in parallel with a search for a co-producer who could help fund the show – and obviously there were moments of frustration.

There's always a fairly high turnover of staff within a big organisation, and during those two years I dealt with several producers and script editors – all of whom had to be brought up to speed on what we'd decided or rejected already, and who had their own ideas and questions about the concept. Looking back, those differing views probably made the show stronger, but there were times I felt like there was someone new on the show every week!

Your series is written not only by you, but by other writers. How do you find this process?

In many ways, this is the best part of the process. Writing is obviously a solitary occupation, but screenwriters, unlike novelists or poets, tend to be fairly gregarious. So being able to get together in a room and discuss characters and plot ideas with other talented, enthusiastic writers is fantastic.

Obviously, getting writers together from different parts of the UK for several days is expensive – the main reason, I think, why British television has been slow to adopt the US 'writers' room' approach to writing – so we have to compromise. Usually we have two or three meetings a season, lasting a couple of days, and thrash out a few episodes at a time.

This involves creating a character arc for the season, mapping the changes we want to see happen in each of our lead characters, and then finding stories that will create that change.

Obviously, by season two, you have actors in place, and you can start writing to their strengths – for example, discovering that one of our cast could sing, and that another studied martial arts, triggered a couple of episode ideas this season. You also get a sense of which characters work unexpectedly well together, and can start creating subplots for them.

Inside the writers' room, everyone is encouraged to throw in ideas, and things can get boisterous – there was a long and heated debate about the morality of a big decision that a character takes in season two! But it's not about egos. Everyone is trying to find the most interesting, dramatic and effective way to tell the story and serve the characters – and if people argue their point passionately, that's a good thing. It makes the show stronger.

I believe script editors are the unsung heroes of television drama production. Can you talk a bit about the script editor's job during the development of *Wolfblood*?

Now this I agree with: script editors *are* the unsung heroes of television. I've been lucky to have worked with great script editors on all the shows I've done so far, and our *Wolfblood* team are particularly brilliant.

The script editor's job is basically to take the story the writer wants to tell, and guide them to tell it in the most effective, dramatic, and achievable way possible. They become a kind of external critical faculty for the writer, someone who can take a step back and say, 'That's a great subplot, but if you gave it to this character instead and moved that scene to here, it would be much more effective.'

The strangest thing about writing is that it's incredibly hard to see the parts of your script that aren't working properly – even things that you'd notice in a heartbeat if you were reading someone else's script! The script editor is there to provide the objective viewpoint that you're too close to the material to provide – and to stand in for the audience, providing that fresh pair of eyes, making sure that your intentions are clear and nothing has been lost or muddied in the rewrites.

They also handle a lot of issues of continuity and tone. In the US, the showrunner would probably rewrite every script by a writer other than himself, to ensure a consistent tone and feel across the series. Here, the script editor works with the writers during the rewrites to achieve that consistency, taking a load off the lead writer's shoulders.

A good script editor also has one eye on the practicalities of budget, casting, scheduling and locations, meaning you don't have to worry too much about that at script stage. If your editor says it can be done, it probably can!

THE CONTINUING FORMAT:
WHAT IT TEACHES WRITERS

Currently, there are precious few single slots available in television schedules for producers to fill and writers to write for. But the wheel goes round and, via the fragmentation and diversification of drama production for the small screen, the dramatic form of television drama is bound to return to the single format once again, with the single television play applauded as a way of exploring our lives, just as it was back in its heyday during the sixties and seventies. This will appeal to a niche market, and the single will no doubt sit like a self-contained morsel amidst a feast of long-running formats, but it will have its place and rightly so.

That's a little way into the future. Not far, but still a way. The fact remains that most writers working in television today do so on established, long-running formats. This is where the majority of the work is, where the most writer contracts are signed, where the most television hours are made, and where, in the main, a writer can truly become a seasoned, creative professional who not only wields a ton of necessary experience in writing for the small screen, but who also enjoys regular writing gigs.

That is not to say that writers I have worked with on drama juggernauts like *Holby City* or *EastEnders* didn't do other projects/ develop other ideas for theatre, or radio, or film. The successful ones all did just that. They were busy. They had a work ethic and a need to write other characters, explore new themes, keep developing their own personal voice; and this, in my view, is an essential thing to do.

Remember, it was the strength of your own voice and your ability to tell a story via the craft of screenwriting that got you your first gig on a series, so it is to this original spark that you should periodically return to keep yourself writing as well as you can.

However, the LRS (long-running series) or LF (long-form) drama forms the backbone of our television schedules and it is this format that can teach writers the most about how to construct and tell a dramatic story for the small screen.

NAIL YOUR STORYLINE

Writing for drama series or serials works the storylining muscle like no other format. Writers have to learn how to create, construct and sell their storylines quickly, with creative flair, and be in control of the ebb and flow of several story arcs at the same time, across 25–60 minutes of drama per episode. Knowing the elements that make up a great story, and being able to present them in a dramatic, coherent, engaging way, is absolutely key to the craft of storylining for television.

Not all writers have a natural ability to storyline, and thankfully, in television, there are storyliners, script editors and a team of story-savvy people to help those who struggle with taking a storyline forward. However, it serves every writer well to be confident and competent at presenting their ideas.

Being able to write a cracking treatment if you are pitching your own idea as part of the development process, or an equally compelling story outline if you are pitching at Story Conference, is vital to getting your voice heard and your input noted.

Being confident enough in your own ability, and in your 'take' on the show, is also important. If you are both these things, then pitching your storyline idea at Story Conference will be fun rather than freakishly terrifying. Should you be working on a show that does not have Story Conferences (a shorter-run show will not), being able to present, develop and analyse storylines is still an essential skill television writers should have.

BE STRUCTURALLY SOLID

Series writing makes a writer up their structure game in record time. If you were the sort of writer who didn't plot out their storylines and scripts before you got the commission to work on a particular show, you'll certainly be the type that does by the time your final payment is made and your script has gone into rehearsal! It pays to plan and be comfortable with handling structural problems in your scripts, and to be able to discuss and make changes in your work as the writing process continues.

BE A PLOTMEISTER

Creating and taming a good plot line goes hand in hand with being adept at handling structure and recognising a good storyline when it comes along. Some television dramas cannot be described as plot-driven (*Gavin and Stacey*, *The 7.39*), whilst others are characterised by their strong plot lines (*Death in Paradise*, *Broadchurch*, *Call the Midwife*); but whether the plot in the work is foregrounded or not, it still needs a writer who can introduce, develop, build and tie up an interesting plot line.

CONTROL THE PACE

Good television writers have an understanding of how an episodic drama should ebb and flow and how the storyline, structure and plotting dictates the pace of the script. Series and serial writing teaches the writer to metre out the storylines across the required length, paying attention to the parts of the story that will need pace and those that can allow the script as a whole to rest up a little. Pacing is a subtle and, in some ways, dark art. If the pace is right in a television script, then the audience will feel they are part of the story on screen, rather than mere passive observers.

CHARACTERISATION

Series dramas have a group of central characters (the ensemble) which can be anything from three or five up to a large regular returning cast (in the case of the established series or soaps) of ten or more. In all cases, the writer is expected to be able to empathise with, and write for, characters they have not created themselves. Being able to quickly get 'an angle' on the characters in a television drama, then, is a useful skill to have. Understanding motivation, the drive of a character, being able to map their journey across the episode and write not just the text that applies to them within their storyline, but their subtext as well, makes a good television writer a great one. Successful television writers, working regularly on series and serial formats are (arguably) the best at understanding character and being able to dig out the essential human qualities – both good and bad – in the characters they write for.

MY EVERGREEN LIST
FOR TELEVISION WRITERS

Storytelling is innate and natural to you because you are a writer. You must learn the craft of how to shape and construct your stories so the industry understands you and wants to work with you.

Set clear goals to achieve within your writing journey. Aim at one single goal at a time; portion off your daily goal, one step at a time, and stick to achieving the end result.

Always be open to criticism as you progress through your writing career. Not everyone will share your opinion of your work, but television is essentially collaborative so giving and receiving criticism is necessary in order to progress. Time will teach you not only how to receive criticism well, but also how to give it.

Be pragmatic in the face of success and failure. It's the only way to be. In private you can gloat or grin inanely at yourself in the morning mirror, but to your public you are a professional writer who fights to keep standards high.

If someone in the industry has given you their time in whatever that way is, for however long it may be, never take that for granted. Always thank those who help you or work with you. Being courteous and considerate even under pressure makes a world of difference to those whose job it is to make your script camera ready.

You write alone, but it takes a whole team of people to make your script part of the ongoing story you see on screen. Make this transition every time you leave your desk and come to the production office.

Believe in yourself. Learn from those around you and stay in touch with what makes you want to write in the first place.

Always find a way to have a laugh at least once a day. Do not get too hung up on your script. It's very important, but so is keeping sane when you are under deadline pressure from the production. Keep a balance in your life.

Do not compare yourself to other writers. Writing is exposing. All writers have insecurities and that goes for the successful ones, too. You are different, and all writers learn and grow at different paces. Believe in your own talent.

Television drama reaches millions of people like you, every day, day after day. To be part of this national process of storytelling takes serious craft, self-belief and an appreciation of what makes us tick as people. Television writers are a solid, gifted, inspirational breed and, if you want to join them, I sincerely hope there is a seat waiting for you around a Story Conference table somewhere soon.

USEFUL **LINKS**

SCREENWRITING TIPS, TRICKS AND LESSONS

Linda Aronson is a powerhouse of all things story and structure related. Her website will take you down a fascinating road where you will discover a whole new way of looking at, and addressing, the problems of narrative structure in films and television drama.
http://www.lindaaronson.com/

Scott Myers is a mine of script-related information, inspiration and practical know-how. His site is definitely one for the bookmark.
http://gointothestory.blcklst.com/2008/09/dumb-little-writing-tricks-that-work-1.html

Elliot Grove established this wonderful festival for all things writing, film and screen related. Raindance hold an annual festival in London, and run courses internationally.
http://www.raindance.org/great-tv-scripts/

Farah Abushwesha is the main contact for BAFTA Rocliffe. This initiative has a great website, and runs a good script competition, and is focused on introducing the industry to emerging film and television talent.
http://www.rocliffe.com/index.php

Charles Harris and his fellow directors run this brilliant website and mentoring company for writers of the big and small screen. They also run practical, inclusive courses in script writing.
http://www.euroscript.co.uk/

Phil Gladwin runs this great site for writers. Sign up for his informative, regular newsletter and enter his script competition. He also runs friendly script courses covering most of the writing craft skill base.
http://www.screenwritinggoldmine.com/

Stephanie Palmer runs her dynamic website, Good in a Room, to serve writers keen to make it across the pond. Her emphasis is on the film industry, but she is great on all things script and story related. Her take on pitching and how to do it well is especially good in my view.
http://www.goodinaroom.com

The London Screenwriters' Festival:
I chaired a forum on writing for soaps in 2012 for this impressive festival, and will happily be back in October 2014 to run another session on the television long-form format. I recommend it for writers who are dipping their feet into the whole screenwriting scene. Notable producers, directors and agents come to this annual gathering in Regent's Park. Their list of speakers gets more luminary each passing year.
http://www.londonscreenwritersfestival.com/

FORMATTING SCRIPTS, DOWNLOADABLE SCRIPTS

Download television scripts from this site – a great one to bookmark for reference: *https://sites.google.com/site/tvwriting/*

Practical, easy to assimilate site for all things format related:
http://creativegenius.hubpages.com/hub/Format-a-New-Screenplay

The Script Lab is a useful site to bookmark – here you can download some truly notable screenplays from 2013:

http://thescriptlab.com/screenwriting-101/screenplay/download-scripts/2435-2013-script-downloads

Keep up with what's what and who's who in the film and television industry here:
http://www.theknowledgeonline.com/guides/post/2013/09/17/A-guide-to-writing-for-TV-drama

BOOKS ON SCREENWRITING

John Yorke: *Into the Woods: A Five Act Journey Into Story*
John's fascination with story and the on-screen narrative is clearly apparent from the first chapter to the last. A great book to keep by your bed, for dipping into on narrative dry days.

Julian Friedmann: *The Insider's Guide to Writing for Television*
This is a direct, no-nonsense book full of really good advice on dealing with contracts, sourcing agents, getting your work out there and fulfilling a TV writing brief. He quotes me on writing for series television, too.

Linda Aronson: *The 21st Century Screenplay*
Everything you know already, thought you knew, and wish you knew more about, here, in one book. Linda is a force of nature. She has an explanation and a description for every structure ever used in the telling of stories for the big and small screen.

ANTONY AND CLEOPATRA:
SCRIPT PAGES BY SALLY WAINWRIGHT

I mention Sally's work a fair bit in this book. Writer clients, friends and colleagues know only too well how highly I rate her writing. I find it always subtle. She has an amazing control of subtext, a sensitive ear to nuance in dialogue. I have had the pleasure of developing projects with Sally back in my Granada TV days; ours never made it to the higher plain of a network commission, but thankfully (and clearly in no need of help from me) she has since had a series of successes with her work. Here, she has kindly allowed me to use the first 14 pages of her original draft for *Last Tango in Halifax*, entitled in its infancy *Antony and Cleopatra*.

<u>SCRIPT TITLE</u>

Written by

Name of First Writer

Based on, If Any

Address
Phone Number

ANTONY AND CLEOPATRA

Episode One

by Sally Wainwright

1   INT. POSH TEA-SHOP, HARROGATE. DAY 1.   1

Saturday morning.

WILLIAM ELLIOT (17, lanky, bookish, glasses) sits
reading/hiding behind the Arden Shakespeare edition of *Antony
and Cleopatra*. He has a shoe shop bag beside him - his reason
for being dragged out shopping today. He's with his mum,
CAROLINE, a respectable, professional-looking 46-year-old
Yorkshire woman, and his grandma, CELIA, a respectable, 74-
year-old Yorkshire woman. They sip coffee. CELIA has
forgotten WILLIAM's there, and so begins a conversation she
probably wouldn't have in front of him.

>   CELIA
> I'd never have been able to bring
> him somewhere like this, you see.
> Your dad.

CAROLINE has the joyless manner of someone who is permanently
preoccupied.

>   CAROLINE
> No.

Pause.

>   CELIA
> He'd dribble.
>   (CAROLINE absorbs this;
>   doesn't respond)
> I tried to keep him neat. If we
> went to like the cafe in
> Sainsbury's. I'd sit with my back
> to the wall and him facing me. Well
> I had to. It's off putting for
> folk. Isn't it? If they've come out
> for a coffee. Seeing someone like
> that. You're feeling sorry for him,
> aren't you?

>   CAROLINE
> No I was [just] -

>   CELIA
> Yeah, well don't. I looked after
> him. And it's more than he'd have
> done for me. Did I tell you about
> the pension?

                    CAROLINE
Yes.

                    CELIA
No provision for me.

                    CAROLINE
No.

                    CELIA
He'd be thinking I'd go first.

                    CAROLINE
Yes [but] –

                    CELIA
But what?

                    CAROLINE
It's not like you're without. Is
it?

                    CELIA
That isn't the point. I didn't
register with him. At all. I was an
inconvenience. For fifty years.
        (she sniggers
        humourlessly, shakes her
        head)
Fifty years.

                    CAROLINE
        (quiet)
Well. He's dead now. So.

                    CELIA
You never liked him.
        (CAROLINE doesn't respond)
I can make better coffee than this
in the microwave.
        (she squints at her own
        lenses)
These glasses are mucky.
        (a pause. She taps her
        fingernails on the table.
        Then –)
I've got a pen-pal. Did William
tell you?

For the first time CAROLINE seems engaged. A quick glance at
WILLIAM.

                    CAROLINE
No.

                CELIA
This fella I was at school with.
Well except he was a lad then,
obviously.

               WILLIAM
I showed Gran how to put her
details on Friends Reunited.

              CAROLINE
So... well who is he?

                CELIA
Alan. He was called. Well, he still
is.

2   EXT. FAR SLACK FARM, RIPPONDEN. DAY 1.   2

An elderly Landrover laden with stuff drives towards the
farm, and pulls up. GILLIAN (43), RAFF (16) and ALAN (74)
step out and unload Morrisons bags from the back; they've
been on their big Saturday morning shop. GILLIAN's just
getting on board with some big information that ALAN and RAFF
seem party to. The conversation is energetic. You have to be
very determined to get a word in edgeways with GILLIAN and
RAFF. We get a sense that the life they live is all a bit
rough and ready. There couldn't be a more marked contrast
between these people and the last lot we've just seen.

              GILLIAN
Hang on. Stop. Start again.
You've...?

               RAFF
When Grandad was at school -

              GILLIAN
He can talk for himself.

               ALAN
         (reluctant but amused)
When I was at school there was this
lass, this girl -

               RAFF
Who he fancied.

               ALAN
Whatever.

              GILLIAN
Keep going.

ALAN thought there was more to say, but now he's put it into
words, that seems to be it. He's smiling. ALAN's always
smiling. Our abiding image of him should be of a man smiling.

                    ALAN
Well that's it really.

                    RAFF
No it isn't. I put his name on
Friends Reunited, right -

                    ALAN
Oh yeah, that's it -

                    RAFF
And there she was. Celia Dawson.

                    ALAN
Nee Armitage.

                    RAFF
Her and Doreen Wilkinson.

                    ALAN
Just two of 'em. Out of the whole
year.

                    GILLIAN
You're joking.

                    RAFF
So we wrote to her.

                    GILLIAN
'We'?

                    RAFF
Grandad were a bit nervous.

                    GILLIAN
What for!?

                    ALAN
Well I were in two minds.

                    GILLIAN
So you wrote to her, and -

                    ALAN
And she wrote back. And we've kept
it going, and...
        (thoughtful, smiling)
Yeah.
        (beat)
It's all nowt.

3   INT. CAFE, HARROGATE. DAY 1.   3

        As before.

                    CELIA
             (casually dismissive)
        It's all nowt.

4   EXT. FAR SLACK FARM. DAY 1.   4

                    ALAN
        We're just pen pals.

5   INT. CAFE, HARROGATE. DAY 1.   5

                    CELIA
        Except it's been a trip down memory
        lane. Well, sort of. Given that –

                    CAROLINE
        Given that...
             (smiling, engaged)
        you're not exactly sure which one
        he is.

                    CELIA
        Well you see he was in my year, but
        not in my form.

                    WILLIAM
        Gran was in the A stream.

                    CELIA
        And if he's who I *think* he is, not
        everything he says adds up. You
        see, I think they lived up in the
        wilds, somewhere up Stainland.

6   EXT. FAR SLACK FARM. DAY 1.   6

     As before.

                    ALAN
        She lived in t'next street.

7   INT. CAFE, HARROGATE. DAY 1.   7

                    CELIA
        Only he talks like he lived in the
        next street. And if he did... well
        I'm beggared if I can place him.

8   EXT/INT. FAR SLACK FARM. DAY 1.   8

     ALAN, GILLIAN and RAFF head inside the farmhouse with the
     supermarket bags.

                    ALAN
I were amazed when she wrote back.
I didn't think I were t'sort
somebody like her'd remember.

          GILLIAN
Why, what sort's she?

          RAFF
Glamorous.

          GILLIAN
     (wry)
Oh aye.

          ALAN
     (fond)
Well, she allus seemed a bit better
spoken ner t'rest. And I was always
on t'shy side. And gormless, so –

          GILLIAN
So where is she now?

          ALAN
Harrogate. She has a little flat.
At her daughter's house.

          RAFF
Last time he saw her was in 1951.

          GILLIAN
Really?

          ALAN
     (nods)
Her dad got a job down in
Sheffield, and that was it. Off
they went.

          RAFF
He was heart-broken.

          GILLIAN
Did she know you had a thing about
her?

          ALAN
     (wistful)
She'd not have looked at me twice.

GILLIAN's not sure she likes the sound of this woman.

          RAFF
I've told him, he wants to invite
himself over.
          (ALAN shakes his head,
          smiling)
               (MORE)

                         RAFF (CONT'D)
               Why not? Say you're passing. Say
               you're in Harrogate anyway, and
               would she like to meet up for a cup
               of tea.

A big black shiny Mitsubishi Warrior pulls up outside.
There's a couple of motocross bikes strapped in the back.
GILLIAN's heart sinks and her face hardens. It's almost
through gritted teeth she says -

                         GILLIAN
               You're Uncle Robbie's here, Raff.

                         RAFF
               Yess!!

                         GILLIAN
                    (mumbles, annoyed)
               Half an hour early.

ALAN's face falls a little too as RAFF grabs his crash helmet
and his kit bag with his leathers in.

                         GILLIAN (CONT'D)
               I want you back by five.

RAFF heads outside. GILLIAN goes with him. No pause in the
conversation.

                         RAFF
               No way!

9   EXT. FAR SLACK FARM. CONTINUOUS. DAY 1.   9

ROBBIE (mid-40's) steps out of his silly big car. He wears
reflective ski sun glasses and a baseball cap. He chews gum
and walks like he's just spent five hours on horseback. We
should feel that GILLIAN is over reacting slightly -

                         GILLIAN
               I told you this last time, I made
               it clear - !

                         RAFF
               Mum! It doesn't *finish* while five!
               How we gonna be *back* here by five?
               Hiya Robbie!

                         ROBBIE
                    (a casual greeting)
               Raff.

We cut back inside...

10   INT. KITCHEN, FAR SLACK FARM. CONTINUOUS. DAY 1.   10

...where ALAN observes things from a safe distance, and with
anxiety. It's rare not to see ALAN smiling.

              GILLIAN
            (to ROBBIE, OOV)
        He has homework.

              RAFF
            (OOV)
      I've done it.

              GILLIAN
            (OOV)
      When?

              RAFF
            (OOV)
      Most of it. I'll do t'rest
      tomorrow.

We cut back to GILLIAN outside -

11   EXT. FAR SLACK FARM. CONTINUOUS. DAY 1.   11

              GILLIAN
      You're working at t'garage all day
      tomorrow and then you'll be saying
      you're knackered!

              RAFF
      I won't.

              GILLIAN
            (to ROBBIE)
      I want him back by *five*.

              ROBBIE
            (cool, indifferent,
             opening his door to get
             back in)
      Right.

              GILLIAN
      No, not 'right' like you're just
      saying it to shut me up. 'Right'
      like you've heard what I've said
      and it's sunk in.

ROBBIE's expression behind his dark glasses never alters.

              ROBBIE
      Right.

ROBBIE gets into the vehicle and shuts his door. RAFF gets in
and lowers the passenger window.

                          RAFF
              I'll ring yer.

The Mitsubishi lurches forward and out of the yard. Loud
music blares from the state-of-the-art 8-speaker hi-fi. We
linger on GILLIAN; on her dislike and mistrust of ROBBIE. She
mumbles something that looks a bit like "bastard" under her
breath.

12   EXT. CAROLINE'S HOUSE, HARROGATE. DAY 1.   12

CELIA, CAROLINE and WILLIAM drive through a leafy suburb of
Harrogate.

                          CAROLINE
              Why don't you ask him for a photo?
              If you can't picture him.

                          WILLIAM
              She's got one.

                          CELIA
              He's sent one. On the email. Only
              I'm none the wiser. Folk change so
              much, don't they? Especially men.

CAROLINE's car pulls into the drive. The house is a
desirable, well maintained detached property, with a bungalow
built onto the main house at a right angle, so (at the back,
which we might not see here) the two properties overlook each
other. There are two other cars in the drive; CELIA's little
runaround, and a slightly elderly BMW, the presence of which
seems to surprise CAROLINE, CELIA and WILLIAM. In a bad way.

                          CELIA (CONT'D)
              John's car.

Cut to a few moments later, as we see WILLIAM and CAROLINE
approach the main house, and CELIA go off to her own private
entry into the granny flat.

13   INT. CAROLINE'S HOUSE, SITTING ROOM. DAY 1.   13

WILLIAM comes in the house first, followed by CAROLINE. JOHN
(46, a good-looking, charismatic academic) appears in the
doorway of the sitting room. LAWRENCE (15, a blond haired
rugby player) Caroline's other son, appears from behind him.

                          LAWRENCE
              Dad's here.

JOHN's nervous, polite, self-effacing, plausible. There's a
tense atmosphere.

                          JOHN
              Hi.

> CAROLINE
> Hello.

> JOHN
> I let myself in.

> CAROLINE
> (indifferent, polite)
> So I see.

> JOHN
> (trying for a smile)
> Hi Will.

JOHN's presence embarrasses WILLIAM. He addresses CAROLINE in a mumble.

> WILLIAM
> I'm off upstairs.

He heads past her and upstairs. CAROLINE waits until WILLIAM's door has closed.

> CAROLINE
> I didn't know you had a key.

> JOHN
> D'you want it back?

CAROLINE can't decide whether to say yes or no. Yes sounds too bitter. No sounds like she's throwing the doors wide open to him.

> CAROLINE
> Either way.

> JOHN
> How's your mother?

> CAROLINE
> Fine.

> JOHN
> Good.

Pause.

> CAROLINE
> (casual, light)
> Why're you here?

> JOHN
> (to LAWRENCE)
> D'you want to give us a few
> minutes?

> LAWRENCE
> Sure.

Happy LAWRENCE clears off. JOHN has the bewildered manner of
an articulate man suddenly unable to say what he needs to
say.

>   JOHN
>   Erm. I'm tempted to say it's a long
>   story. But it isn't really. In fact
>   it's pretty straight forward. Turns
>   out... Judith's a bit of an
>   alcoholic.

14   INT. SITTING ROOM, CELIA'S FLAT. DAY 1.   14

CELIA's taking her coat off. Disliking herself for doing it,
she surreptitiously pushes the Venetian blind apart slightly
to see if she can see anything going on in CAROLINE's sitting
room. From her POV, we see CAROLINE follow JOHN into the
sitting room. CAROLINE invites JOHN to sit down.

15   INT. SITTING ROOM, CAROLINE'S HOUSE. DAY 1.   15

CAROLINE remains standing.

>   JOHN
>   I knew she had a
>   (wry)
>   'significant relationship' with the
>   stuff. I knew she 'liked a drink'.
>   But erm... yeah.
>   (CAROLINE has a mixture of
>   disgust and indifference
>   on her face)
>   Didn't realise the extent of it.

CAROLINE fights the urge to say something along the lines of
"So what?"

>   CAROLINE
>   Has she tried to get help?

>   JOHN
>   Oh yeah. More than once. I don't
>   think it's something that'll sort
>   itself out over night. Well, if
>   ever. In fact. So. Yup.

CAROLINE thinks her response through carefully. The tone of
it. She's careful not to sound at all vindictive or smart.

>   CAROLINE
>   And so how does this involve me?

>   JOHN
>   I've made a terrible mistake,
>   Caroline.

Pause.

>   CAROLINE
> Oh. I see.
>   (she's thoughtful.
>   Eventually...)
> You want to come back.

>   JOHN
>   (delicately, hardly daring
>   to ask)
> What d'you think?

>   CAROLINE
>   (genuine; quiet)
> I don't know.

>   JOHN
> I was dazzled. It's pathetic, isn't
> it? Even more so when you see what
> a ridiculous, empty-headed mess
> she...
>   (dries up)
> Sorry. You don't want to hear this.
> And so *selfish*. Out of necessity, I
> suppose. You can't imagine it 'til
> you've...
>   (dries up)
> Sorry. I suppose I never have. Seen
> it before. Up close. The real
> McCoy. And it's only now. I
> realise. How much of a fool I've
> made of myself. And to have thrown
> away all this. Here. With you and
> the boys. And for what? It's
> appalling, it's abysmal. It's
> unthinkable.

Is he on the verge of tears? CAROLINE can see he's genuine.

16   EXT. FAR SLACK FARM. DAY 1.   16

GILLIAN's penned a small flock of sheep in, and she's
scraping out their hooves.

17   INT. FAR SLACK FARM. DAY 1.   17

ALAN's settled down at the computer with a cup of coffee and
the remainder of the packet of Hobnobs that RAFF started on.
He's nervous. He starts writing.

>   ALAN
>   (voice over)
> Dear Celia. I am planning a trip up
> to Skipton next week.
>   (pause)
>   (MORE)

```
                    ALAN (CONT'D)
          Possibly Monday.
               (pause)
          If you fancied meeting up for a
          coffee, it would be a wonderful
          opportunity [to]... Would you fancy
          meeting up for a coffee? A cup of
          coffee. I appreciate that you
          probably have much more interesting
          things to [do]... That you may
          already have your week planned. But
          if you did happen to be available.
          Free. I would be delighted if
          you... it would be very nice to see
          you. With very best wishes...
               (pause)
          Best wishes, Alan.
```

He puts an 'x' after his name, then deletes it again. He
moves the cursor up to send. Just as he's worked up enough
courage to click the mouse, the phone rings. He answers it.

```
                    ALAN (CONT'D)
          Hello?
```

Cutting with:

18   EXT. FIELD. DAY 1.   18

Motorbike engines roar in the background. ROBBIE's on his
mobile. An ambulance. RAFF's on a stretcher being tended by
paramedics. And it looks pretty serious from where ROBBIE's
standing. ROBBIE isn't the cool dude he was earlier. He's
flustered, trying to keep calm.

```
                    ROBBIE
          Alan, it's Robbie. Lad's come off
          his bike. Is Gillian there?

                    ALAN
               (instant panic)
          No, she's -
```

He looks outside by way of completing the sentence. But
ROBBIE's interrupted anyway -

```
                    ROBBIE
          Ambulance is here. They're taking
          him to t'Princess Royal. Shall I
          see you there then, or what?

                    ALAN
          Yeah, but - so what's he done?

                    ROBBIE
          I dunno. He's - he's conscious now
          anyway, so -
```

                    ALAN
                (more alarm)
         We'll see you there. Tata.

ALAN hangs up. His legs have gone a bit weak with the shock.
He turns to the computer, presses the mouse to send the
message before he can think about it too much (almost like
it's part of his panic) then runs to the outer door.

                  ALAN (CONT'D)
    Gillian!!

THE LAST WORD

Writing is hard, but writing well is harder. And writing really good television, under deadline and within the strictures of a particular show and in collaboration with a team of opinionated script people and a (usually) stressed producer, is even harder.

If you think you have the stamina, ideas, skin of required thickness and a well-developed sense of humour, then writing regularly for television is rewarding both creatively and financially.

However, to earn your place around the Story Conference table on a long-running series, or to be commissioned to write on a television serial, you need to be confident in specific areas and bring to that table a selection box of skills.

In this book I have set out to cover the essential areas necessary for you to understand and get a grip on if you want to flourish as a writer in a television environment, and enjoy yourself into the bargain.

I hope you have enjoyed reading and I wish you all the very best of luck with your current writing and your quest to get into television. It's nice work if you can get it and, with this book as a guide, there's no reason why you can't do just that.

SCRIPT ADVICE – HERE TO HELP YOU

Need further help? Please visit my website *www.scriptadvice.co.uk* and I will do my best to make your script the best it can be.

Twitter – find me here and let's connect!
https://twitter.com/YVONNEGRACE1

Facebook – Script Advice Writers' Room

http://www.facebook.com/groups/237330119115/
I set up this group to promote my work and to provide a great place to chat and swap information with like-minded souls. It's one of the best groups on Facebook for writers.

INDEX

About Us

In addition to Creative Essentials, Oldcastle Books has a number of other imprints, including No Exit Press, Kamera Books, Pulp! The Classics, Pocket Essentials and High Stakes Publishing
> oldcastlebooks.co.uk

Checkout the kamera film salon for independent, arthouse and world cinema **> kamera.co.uk**

For more information, media enquiries and review copies please contact Frances **> frances@oldcastlebooks.com**